MIND PHASES

Consciousness and the information processing cycle

LORRAINE McFADDEN PhD

Library and Archives Canada Cataloguing in Publication

McFadden, Lorraine

Mind Phases: Consciousness and the information processing cycle

ISBN: ***978-1-9991876-1-3*** (book)

ISBN: ***978-1-9991876-2-0*** (ebook)

Published by Lorraine McFadden

Graphic Production by Daria Lacy

Cover photo by Br Zp

for Bill

CONTENTS

Introduction

ONE APPEAL of the topic of consciousness is that
it is undefinable, a wildly intractable and seemingly impossible to solve problem. It is the kind
of problem that can occupy a lifetime. I started
thinking about it decades ago as a research assistant in a neurology lab. I wrote my comprehensive paper on it while in graduate school. I finally
had the time to return to it when, as a newly re-
tired neuropsychologist, the pandemic arrived in
Canada and my husband and I began to isolate.

While in the intervening decades the field
of consciousness studies has developed and expanded, there is still acknowledged difficulty in
the neuroscience and philosophy fields with even
defining the topic. The literature in my field of
neuropsychology was limited, and there was no
model of consciousness. I had originally asked
how does a physical organ, the human brain, generate consciousness? The question in my graduate paper became more refined to, how does
awareness break down in brain injury? By the

time I read Harris' 2019 book, Consciousness, the questions were slightly more focussed and certainly more numerous. I started with the tools I had, a PhD and years of experience in Clinical Neuropsychology.

I began with the syndromes of lost awareness in the neuropsychology literature, and the concept that awareness was a cognitive function (Schacter, McAndrews and Moscovitch 1988). From that point onward there was one problem after another. Big, juicy, interesting problems. This book lays out the problems, some answers and a model of cognitive cycles wherein consciousness has a defined function.

The first hurdle to thinking about consciousness is what I think of as the Infinity Pool problem. A person floating in an Infinity Pool cannot see the edge of the pool, but does have the experience of seeing everything: water, horizon and sky with no limits and no boundaries. It is an optical illusion. The experience of consciousness carries the same type of illusion. The conscious mind has a sense of infinite possibilities and no limits. The real world is everything I can see and feel. Of course it is not true. There is much our conscious mind cannot directly sense.

A second problem with understanding consciousness is thinking that it does all the work. We tend to think of the unconscious as a giant library where we store memories and things we have learned, where things are kept quietly on a shelf until we need to call them up. The unconscious library idea is also an illusion. A lot of cognitive activity occurs out of conscious mind, in this unconscious place, and we can not experience this machinery directly. Thinking that the conscious mind is the active, engaged and useful part of cognition is the out of sight, out of mind problem.

A third and associated problem is thinking that what we store in memory, all of our experiences, skills, education and thoughts, is archived pristine and whole in the unconscious. We store a memory in the library where it sits until we need it. If what we recall from memory is not precisely what was initially stored, we view that as a fault of memory. This is not the whole story. The unconscious is an active part of the information processing system. It transforms the information the conscious mind gathers. Information rotates from conscious experience into the unconscious and back to conscious use, and is changed in the process.

A fourth problem is dismissing ideas, inspirations and sudden solutions to problems as some sort of mental magic. These experiences are the evidence of ongoing unconscious cognitive activity. These phenomena demonstrate the ways in which the unconscious mind processes information. It does this automatically and constantly, shifting and resorting information and building our own personal world view. The unconscious mind creates reality and poses questions for the conscious mind.

Consciousness is not, as we tend to think, the whole of reality. It is just a phase one goes through. It is one of a set of mental processes that operates in a cycle of conscious and unconscious phases. Consciousness is the phase of learning. It is where you experience, explore, investigate and analyze the world. The unconscious phase sorts the information gleaned in consciousness and places it in the context of everything you have experienced and learned before. The unconscious builds a gestalt and forms a world view, a set of expectations about how the world operates and what you can expect to happen. It provides you with a degree of conviction about the world. There are some things you will believe and take for granted. There are other things that do not merit full conviction, and in those areas you will consciously experience curiosity and a desire to investigate and explore.

Nature, biology and neuroscience are full of examples of phases that operate in repeating patterns to form cycles. Reproduction is a basic biological example. The Krebs cycle produces energy in a cell. Sleep goes through REM and NonREM cycles. Perhaps consciousness can be usefully viewed as one phase in an information processing cycle.

It is an interesting approach. This book then is an attempt to take that approach and describe consciousness in terms of cyclical cognitive processes. The Infinity Pool section addresses the boundaries of conscious perception. The Loss of Awareness section considers the structure of awareness in consciousness. The Library and Ring of Truth sections look at the products, and reconsider the functions, of the unconscious phase. The Nautilus section similarly reconsiders the exploration and information building functions of the conscious phase. The final section, Consciousness, places consciousness in an information processing and knowledge building cycle.

It is a working model that offers enough structure to consider other phenomena. If consciousness is but one part of a larger information processing mechanism, then it is possible to think of a cognitive cycle as a means to extend our capacity to think, explore and learn. It is where we analyze, but also where we put what we have learned into practice. It allows us to draw on previous learning to plan, create and build. The conscious phase acquires information and does a share of information processing. The unconscious processes take that information and build the reality we consciously inhabit. The conscious phase takes that product and puts it to use. The conscious and unconscious states act together to transform raw sensory data into a complex, believable network of knowledge. If all of that is a workable concept, then it is reasonable to think that the fundamental goal of the cognitive cycle is learning.

Lorraine McFadden PhD ABPP/CN

London, Ontario, Canada

June 2022

Section 1
Awareness and Infinity

Chapter 1: The Infinity Pool

ONCE YOU have learned something new, it recedes from awareness. Using a clutch and shifting gears becomes automatic. Times tables or chess moves become routinized. Finding your way from home to work is mostly autonomous. The experience, skill or information that you consciously worked on is no longer conscious. Are you aware of the point at which it left consciousness, became a part of your body of knowledge, became routine? It is unlikely. Awareness can not cross the border between the conscious and unconscious minds. It does not have direct access to the contents of the unconscious mind. There is a hard boundary preventing consciousness access to the unconscious mind, but we are unable to perceive that boundary, or even that a boundary exists.

Trying to describe something for which there is no awareness is elusive. It is much like asking a patient with neglect to look to the left. You will be met with puzzlement. Left? What is left? There is no left. There is no there, there. Try to imagine

"

what the boundary between your conscious mind and your unconscious might look or feel like.

The closest approximation I can think of to this experience is the infinity pool. An infinity pool is a type of water or swimming pool, with three normal edges. The fourth side is built to be lower than the other three sides. The depth of the water matches the height of the fourth wall. Water in the pool is continuously pumped in so that the water level rises and pours over the fourth side like a waterfall. Below the edge of the fourth side is a catch basin. The water overflow is collected here, and then pumped back in from the bottom of the pool.

Imagine that you are floating in the pool with just your head above water. You are always facing the fourth side. From this vantage point you can not see the edge on the fourth side. You see the surface of the water and the sky beyond, with no discernible boundary. This is the visual illusion of infinity. There is sky above you, reflected in the water. The water flows in constant circulation, from the pool to the edge and then gone.

This is a model for the illusion of consciousness. The water flow is information, captured like the image from the sky onto the surface of the water. The water flow is constant but the movement is invisible from your point of view. Every part of the flow of information, with the exception of that one part on the surface, is beyond awareness. As far as you, in the infinity pool, are concerned, the surface of the pool and the sky is all there is; the entire world.

To stretch the metaphor until it squeaks, the sky reflected in the water is akin to information acquired in the conscious mind. The flow of water, or information, is automatic and beyond your control. What you can see is determined by the structure of the pool and your position in it. The contents of awareness are determined by the limited scope of attention. Awareness is restricted in range and span. That awareness can focus in different directions does not mean it has a full access pass.

The infinity pool metaphor illustrates the inability to appreciate the terminal point of consciousness. It also illustrates the difference between awareness and consciousness.

To consider this concept further I want to discuss the difference between consciousness and awareness. Consciousness is being awake and alert, able to interact meaningfully with the environment. Awareness is the point of focussed attention, of what one is aware. I think of awareness as the subject of the matter and consciousness as the context. Awareness is the task at hand, consciousness is the background. One can be fully conscious and yet not see the gorilla marching across the stage.

In the infinity pool, awareness is the head above water, seeing water's surface and the whole sky but not the edges or into the water below. Awareness ends at the sky but consciousness takes up at that point and provides a predictive context. The infinity pool describes awareness, but consciousness is the water in which you float.

On a more abstract level, your internal monologue, the running stream of stray thoughts and ideas, is the mental equivalent of the water. In real world terms, you may not need to attend right now to something, but thoughts are quietly active in consciousness and outside of awareness. You do not need to get ready for an appointment or zoom call right now, but you will in half an hour, and that thought is residing in consciousness. It will be pulled into awareness the closer you get to the appointed time. Your child is playing quietly in the next room, so you do not need to attend right now, but part of your conscious mind is tuned to them and any event, even too much silence, that might require your full attention.

So, the conscious mind is quite active, queuing future events and readying itself to bring things to awareness as needed. The aware mind is devoted to the task in front of it but operates in a context of other stray items that might, or will, need attention. To return to the infinity pool metaphor, awareness is looking up and out but it also knows it is in a pool of water. It is aware of the surface of the water, and it is aware things can and will bubble up to the surface. When they do, they will enter into full awareness, but the task of the aware mind is to be always looking outward.

Awareness does not readily grasp this boundary. This curious sense of an unknown reality has two implications. One is an implicit acknowledgement of an unconscious mind. It is the name we apply to any material we do not consciously access. Something is there alright, but it is unreachable and therefore unknown. The other is curiosity. This seems to play out in the real world as a drive to explore the unknown, a fascination with mystery, a compulsion to understand.

The experience of information making a transition from the conscious to the unconscious mind has no vocabulary. We do not have words for the experience of, say, the point at which operating a clutch on a manual transmission becomes automatic and no longer requires conscious monitoring of the process, or when typing on a keyboard goes from every move is effortful and intentional to a smooth and efficient flow. In retrospect, that the transition occurred is obvious, but the process happens automatically, outside of awareness, without being experienced.

I wonder if human curiosity is our response to this sense of unknown material beyond an invisible limit. Linking human curiosity to the limits of awareness is a useful construct because it sets in motion the possibility of a cycle of information acquisition and transmission.

Such a hypothetical cycle could start with curiosity. It can then be thought of as a drive to bring more experience, skill or information into awareness. Once in awareness, the raw data of the new thing can be processed with cognitive functions such as attention, language and memory. The new thing is transformed into information, which can be learned and stored. Once the information has been processed and it has receded into the unconscious, there is a void in the frame of attention. Curiosity returns to to seek out more.

This sort of exchange of information is very much like any gradient in physics or chemistry. Water flows downhill; ions cross a membrane to reach equilibrium. The movement of water or ions or information will continue as long as there is an imbalance. If the conscious mind can never perceive the volume of information in the unconscious, and everything it acquires recedes to hidden storage, could this be a mechanism that perpetuates curiosity and learning? Will such a mechanism seek out and process more experience? Will it keep sending information down that one way gradient?

In biology, few such mechanisms are strictly one way. They form part of a cycle in which, for example, ions pass one way through a membrane at one part of the cycle, to re emerge elsewhere. The flow perpetuates the cycle. In the infinity pool metaphor, the water flows over the edge, to be caught in the overflow pool and pumped back into the pool.

The drive to satisfy curiosity, to learn anything, to go anywhere new, to do something new whether it is an experience, skill or knowledge, does not seem to be under our volitional control. Yes, we intentionally learn new things, but the reason we do decide to experiment, ask questions or explore is not under our control. Have you ever tried to not be curious about something? It is like not thinking about pink elephants. It is like closing the mystery novel on the penultimate page, saying, "No, I don't want to know how it turns out." Curiosity is automatic, and once engaged, it proceeds.

That curiosity is a non volitional, perhaps automatic, function suggests a mechanism that drives curiosity, and consequently the conscious process of acquiring and processing information. In that case, the reason that the conscious mind has no awareness of the process is because it does not need to know anything about the process, the limits or the unconscious. No such information is needed if the job is just to find and process something new. If the drive for information is innate and not volitional, then there is no need to expend conscious resources on anything other than knowledge acquisition.

That in turn suggests the interesting idea that consciousness is part of an automatic information gathering and processing mechanism.

Awareness has been likened to a flashlight beam, wherein the experience of awareness is restricted to just what is within that small wedge of light (Baars, 2005, 2017). Again, like the infinity pool, it suggests that the range and span of attention in awareness is quite limited. Awareness seeks out the unknown for analysis. Beyond that cognitive function lies a range of mental processes that operate automatically on the newly processed information. What we know of implicit cognitive operations suggests that this stage of acquiring information is only a small segment of a larger mental operation.

So, we have awareness and consciousness seeking out and processing raw sensory data into information. The information recedes from awareness. We think of it as stored in the unconscious. Is that it? Are we just perpetually stocking an information larder?

Perhaps there is an information cycle at work. If we follow information as it is processed cognitively from awareness to unconsciousness, is there an indication of an outflow of information elsewhere?

Subsequent chapters look at the ways in which stored information is recycled into awareness. One significant mental process is called prediction. This is a body of knowledge about what should be in the real world. It provides a set of expectations (the sun rises in the morning, your spouse will still have the same name, the laws of physics are still operating) and some automatic responses to everyday events (such as greeting co-workers). In the conscious mind lies a prediction of what should be and what to expect. Prediction is a very useful mental function in that it frees up the limited attentional resources of awareness to deal with the things that require attention.

The literature on prediction theory is extensive, but Barrett's (2020) Seven and a Half Lessons About the Brain is a good place to start.

Prediction is an interesting concept. It appears to act by building a model of what should be, and what to expect of the territory in consciousness but not in the immediate focus of attention, the area of awareness. This is the peripheral visual field, the subliminal auditory and visual range, where attention is not focussed but is on stand by to respond to novelty. What sort of resources would it take to create such a mirage?

First of all, it would have to be made up of knowledge of what could be there, and that knowledge is acquired in real life experience. What is going on in that period of time before you have amassed enough information to build a model about what is out there? I would surmise an intense period of information gathering. It is reminiscent of the early life phase Gopnik (2020) calls the Explorer Consciousness.

It seems reasonable to assume that the prediction function is always on during consciousness. Are there times when prediction is not operating as expected? If ever you had the experience, upon wakening, of not known where you are, and taken a moment to orient yourself, could this be a lag in the prediction function coming on line? Is prediction operating in the case of a newborn with no world experience to draw upon?

Does this prediction function require resources in order to operate efficiently? It seems a reasonable assumption, in view of what we know about cognitive functions: they take energy.

To come at the question from a different angle, are there any alterations in consciousness associated with a serious depletion of energy? Amongst some cultures there are practices whereby people deliberately put themselves into prolonged periods of limited food and water, sometimes known as a spirit quest, in order to induce experiences of altered consciousness. Prolonged periods of fasting, silence and stillness can induce such experiences. Prolonged lack of sleep can induce hallucinatory experiences. Explorers on the edge of exhaustion, alone and in significant energy deprivation, have reported specific types of hallucination, known as the third man experience (Pearson, 2014). These are cases in which the normal consciousness changes. A hypothesis of a breakdown in the prediction function provides a model for occurrences that otherwise can only be labelled strange.

There are other situations in which, due to illness, neurodegenerative process or injury, that a breakdown in prediction occurs. They can be described as delusions and hallucinations. Sometimes the person experiencing them is aware the hallucinations are not real, but not always. There is the curious disorder of delusional misidentification syndromes, such as Capgras syndrome and reduplicative paramnesia, which is a false belief in duplicates and doubles. Early on in my work as a research assistant a patient came into hospital with a parietal lobe stroke. He was admitted to the Stroke Unit and occupied one of four beds. He was awake and alert, but held the belief that he was at home, in his basement, which had been set up as a Stroke Unit. Years later in my practice I assessed a gentleman who was experiencing hallucinations arising from a neurodegenerative disorder. He was aware the hallucinations were not real, but they were disturbing, and he tried to avoid looking at them by turning his head.

The question of what consciousness does yields a very interesting picture of cycles of cognitive processes. What we know, for example of learning and memory, is that cognitive processes operate before and after information is stored in the unconscious. We know that awareness can be altered in a variety of ways by a focal injury, such as a stroke, in the brain. We have seen that awareness of the world is a focussed, directed activity of the brain. It enables very specific cognitive activities in consciousness. In subsequent chapters we will see that much of the information processing that the brain performs in the realms of emotion, thought and skill, is unconscious. The unconscious mind is able to take the information the conscious mind has acquired and generate ongoing, detailed predictions about the world around us. Those predictions are so complete and subtle that they effectively generate a mirage, an illusion of what we expect to experience in the world at large. The unconscious prepares us for what responses to the environment we might require. When the prediction fails, and something unexpected occurs, we focus our attention and respond consciously.

The next chapter will look at what we do know of the ways in which awareness functions by how it breaks down after brain injury.

Chapter 2: Loss of Awareness

THERE IS a technique in archaeology called field walking. An archaeologist walks a field to see what has been turned up after plowing. The artifacts sitting on the surface provide clues to what lies below. It might be a pot, a wall, a structure. As the saying goes in archaeology, "two stones make a feature, three stones make a wall".

Like field walking, neuropsychology tries to recreate the original structure of a cognitive function from behavioural changes after localized brain injury such as a stroke. A great deal is known about how language is functionally organized in the brain from persons who have suffered a stroke that affects their use of language. If that can be achieved with language, can we do the same with awareness?

It turns out the answer is yes. There are a number of highly specific ways in which awareness is altered following brain damage. Awareness of a body part, or the left side of space or even awareness of the ability to see can all be lost.

Many years when I was a research assistant in a neurology lab, a woman came into hospital following a stroke that affected the posterior parts of her brain. Both left and right occipital lobes were involved. She developed a case of cortical blindness, meaning the visual cortex in her brain was not functioning, but the rest of the visual system, including her eyes, was unaffected. Because some of the vision regions in her brain could not process visual information, she was effectively blind from the stroke. The curious aspect was that she was unaware that she could not see. To overcome this inexplicable problem, she confabulated various scenarios to help her explain why she could not see things she thought she should be able to see. She would claim the blinds in her room were closed, and because of the darkness she could not make out how many people were in the room. She could not directly articulate a problem she did not know she had.

It is challenging to grasp this syndrome. We are accustomed to being aware of the things we do and experience. We assume the two cognitive activities, function and awareness, are one, conjoined, indivisible. If I walk across a room, I am aware that I do so. If I pick up a coffee cup or plan a shopping trip tomorrow, I am aware of what I touch, write and think. But this sort of awareness of everyday activities can be lost in neurological disease or injury. In these cases, the affected person is not unconscious; they remain aware of everything except one specific aspect of their existence.

The opposite problem can also occur. It is possible, in some cases of stroke or injury, to retain some visual capacity but yet to have the sensation of blindness. Such patients believe they are blind. Visual information still guides their behaviour, but they are not aware of what they see. A case reported by Gelder et al (2008) is a good example. A patient presented to hospital with a stroke to the back of the brain, on both left and right sides. When examined, the patient reported he was completely blind. During his stay, the doctors observed him walking down a corridor in the hospital. He approached a chair in the hall and then walked around it, thus avoiding the obstacle. He was asked how he had seen the chair, but the patient denied seeing anything. He continued to say he was blind. He could not account for why he had walked around the obstacle he had not seen.

The physicians devised an experiment. They set up an obstacle course in a hallway, full of objects a blind person would stumble into, but laid out in a way a sighted person could navigate. They arranged to have people stationed near the obstacles so that if the patient did bump into them, he would not fall. They then brought the patient in and asked him to walk down the corridor. He navigated the obstacles without bumping or stumbling. Although he reported blindness, he showed no awareness of any visual information. He reported no other problems. The stroke had altered his awareness of vision, but left all other systems unaffected.

The changes these patients experienced have important implications. First, such cases linked a localized brain lesion to a circumscribed loss of awareness. Awareness was not a global perception of the world; it could operate in just one sensory system at a time. Second, although there have been multiple reports of such changes in awareness, the lesions are not in the same region of the brain. There is no single area of the brain devoted to awareness. Third, awareness seems to be a specialized mode of function in the brain. It operates normally for some cognitive tasks, such as vision, but not for all brain activities. There are many brain functions that work outside of awareness. You do not consciously jerk your knee when a doctor taps it with a hammer. The reflex is automatic and not consciously willed. The mechanics of digestion occur without your will or awareness. Fourth, the normal awareness we enjoy every day can fail for just one function and leave the rest unaffected.

The terms consciousness and awareness are sometimes used interchangeably. There are subtle but important differences between the two. Consciousness is the general term for being awake and alert; awareness is a specific term for the experience of consciousness. In medicine and neuropsychology, consciousness is defined with behaviours. For example, one widely used measure is the Glasgow Coma Scale, and it is used to determine where someone's level of consciousness lies on a scale from 3 (lowest) to 15 (highest). Three types of response to command are tested:

best eye response, best verbal response and best motor response. Someone who is opening their eyes spontaneously, able to answer basic questions about who and where they are, and following simple commands like pointing to the door, gets full points and is described as fully conscious. As the ability to function in any of these three areas declines, the Glasgow Coma Scale score drops. Depending on how low the score goes, one's level of consciousness is said to be mildly, moderately or severely compromised. Consciousness is defined, very practically, as being able to interact meaningfully with the environment and other people.

Awareness is a little different. Let's say you are conscious, you know your name, you know it's Tuesday, and you can point to the door. I can determine if you are conscious with observation and some simple commands. The only way I can directly test for awareness is to ask you to tell or show me that you are. In order to determine if you are aware of what just happened, I need to ask you: "Are you aware of what just happened?". Awareness is a subjective state and is not objectively measured by direct means. There are indirect methods, as seen in later sections.

As a clinician I know that, to administer neuropsychological tests, it is necessary for a patient to be fully conscious. Testing is deferred if a patient is not fully awake, alert, oriented and free of intoxicants. Consciousness must be fully functional and available to the task presented to the patient.

If awareness is absent in some modality, alternate testing methods are needed.

The ways in which awareness can fail suggest that it acts like any other cognitive function that can fail. Each cognitive function operates in a domain, with its own tools and limits. For example, language is a domain of function that uses words, grammar and rules to process information in a specific fashion. Awareness uses attention to focus on a specific thing. Once attention has been brought to bear, other cognitive functions come on line and process the specific thing in some fashion. Awareness acts like part of an information processing system. It focuses cognitive functions to process something in terms of, say, its spatial location, shape or colour. Once processed the thing can be stored in memory. Awareness is cognizant only of the very thing in front of its nose, and entrains other cognitive functions to process it for storage.

When fully awake we assume that we are completely aware of ourselves and our environment. We expect that we can sense things normally and move at will. The startling truth is that those assumptions do not hold up very well. For example, we all have a blind spot in our field of vision. It is due to an area at the back of the eye which is just off centre. It is the place where the nerves that line the back of your eye join together and form a bundle, called the optic nerve. There are no visual receptors there. This translates into a blind spot in our visual field corresponding to this place at the back of the eye.

We have no awareness of a blind spot in our vision. The brain predicts what is most likely there and we take the prediction as reality (Barrett, 2020). The brain is providing a powerful illusion, or mirage, to overcome the gap in sensory information. All we have to do to become aware of what is in the blind spot is shift visual focus, and the blind spot shifts away as well. The visual blind spot becomes a metaphor for anything not in our focus of attention.

By shifting visual focus, or the focus of attention, one can also shift awareness. This leads to an interesting effect that occurs when paying attention to one particular thing. In the now famous gorilla experiment, a video of players passing balls back and forth was shown to a group of observers. The video shows six people, three wearing white t shirts and three wearing black t shirts. They move about, constantly passing the balls back and forth amongst themselves. The observers were told their task was to count the number of times a ball was passed between two players wearing white shirts. There is a lot of movement, and counting the passes requires sustained, careful attention. At the end of the video, the observers are asked if they saw the gorilla. About half of the people who are unfamiliar with the experiment do not recall seeing a gorilla, although a person in a gorilla suit walks through the players about half way through the video, pauses, beats its chest, and walks off (Chabras & Simon, 2010). About half of the observers recalled the number of passes and did not observe anything else. The observers also failed to notice the background curtain changing colour, or one of the black shirted players walking off the set.

This is a very interesting thing about awareness. It works in a tight range of focus, but is otherwise quite limited. Like eye witness experiments, in which witnesses demonstrate poor consistency after observing the same scene, we not only do not appreciate everything we observe, we usually have no sense of having missed anything.

The illusion of full awareness of something, such as vision in the blind spot or the events in our eye witness account, is complete and compelling. Our brain manufactures a prediction of what is most plausibly going on elsewhere while we are in the process of paying attention to something. We have no sense of the unreality of the prediction.

The earliest accounts of any loss of awareness after brain injury were documented by Dr. Holmes in 1918 in Britain. Dr. Holmes, a British physician, published an account of his investigations of soldiers wounded during World War I. These accounts described different types of visual defects that arose as a result of wounds to the back of the head, the occipital region. Some of his patients reported altered awareness of their vision. The loss of vision might occur in only a limited part of the visual field, such as the upper, lower, left or right quadrants of the visual field. The loss of vision might occur in some circumstances, but not others. Some alterations were transient, and some persisted. For example, one soldier did not report blindness but he could not identify food placed before him. Another could not read whole words, but was able to sound them out in a letter by letter fashion. One soldier could identify a moving object in his field of vision, but if it stopped moving he could not see it, nor identify it.

Dr. Holmes could only localize the brain damage through external visual inspection of the head wound. There was no CT or MR imaging in 1918, and localizing brain damage in a living person was very basic. These early case studies showed that different lesion locations in the brain were associated with different types of loss of awareness in vision, including functions such as word reading, detection of movement and identification and awareness of visual function.

That is where the curious phenomena of loss of awareness of vision remained until the 1970s, when it was taken up again as a line of research. When Weiskrantz and colleagues began to investigate visual changes in human brain lesion cases in the mid 1970's, it was possible to localize brain damage in more detail using a CT scanner. For example, brain injury in the primary visual cortex was associated in multiple clinical cases with normal visual-guided function despite reports of blindness (Weiskrantz, 2004).

The work of Holmes and Weiskrantz showed that the experience of vision was different than the function of vision. The people in question did not lose vision; they lost their awareness of vision. These findings were replicated by other researchers. "The important point was that subjects seemed to be able to make visual discriminations in the clinically blind fields even though they acknowledged no awareness of them" (Weiskrantz, 2004). Weiskrantz coined the term, 'blindsight' to describe the phenomenom. His work suggested that a great deal of visual information may not be processed consciously.

Ajina and Bridge (2016) pointed out that blindsight did not occur invariably in cases of occipital brain damage, only in some cases. From eye to occipital cortex, there are multiple pathways in the brain that serve different visual based functions, but only some of those pathways terminate in the visual cortex. Only some of the cases of stroke or injury resulted in reports of blindness. The obvious conclusion was that some visual processes occur in awareness, but not all. Some visual information processing, such as avoiding an obstacle in a hallway, may or may not be conscious. For example, you may blink at a sudden stimulus, like an object coming toward your eye, without being aware of the object at all.

This is a simplification of a complex neural system underlying visual functions, but the point is that only some neural pathways are associated with the conscious experience of seeing. Ajina and Bridge (2016) concluded that the brain's processing of shape and form largely occurs in conscious vision. Identifying something in the visual field occurs consciously. *Something is moving* is one visual process and occurs outside of awareness; identifying it, *that is a mouse,* is a different process and it is conscious.

Following on the idea that function and awareness could be separated by an injury to the brain, investigators looked into other cognitive functions and their links to awareness. A major element of such research was the ability to image the brain, using modalities such as CT or MRI, to provide structural information about the brain and the injury. One of the interesting questions was whether or not awareness arose in a specific region of the brain.

That line of questioning concluded that patients may experience cognitive loss after brain injury but such losses do not all map to the same brain regions, for a number of reasons. There are individual differences in brain circuitry. For example, the majority of people are right handed and the majority of people have areas crucial to language in the left hemisphere. A small proportion of people are ambidextrous or left handed, and a small proportion of those people have language functions localized either in the right hemisphere, or both hemispheres. In addition, a specific cognitive activity normally occurs in multiple brain regions acting together, not just a single region.

What do these studies imply about awareness and consciousness?

One way to think of consciousness is as a cognitive function. We used to think of different domains of cognitive function as being localized to a specific brain region, but that is not the whole story. Cognitive functions rely on the integrity of specific brain regions, but the cognitive processing in, for example, language, relies on the involvement of many other regions. So, it might not be a safe assumption to say consciousness is localized to one brain area. A useful aspect of thinking of consciousness as a cognitive function is that cognitive functions can be measured. Performance on neuropsychological tests provides data on how well, or how poorly, a cognitive function is performing. Cognitive functions rely on the integrity not only of specific brain regions, but healthy connectivity to other regions as well. A stroke may occur in a brain region associated with memory, or it may interfere with connections between regions. Because of these variables, performance on memory testing may be better or worse than a brain scan might predict.

Before exploring that further, I would like to clarify some terms. A cognitive function is a way in which the human brain processes information. It is restricted to a specific set of operations and has specific types of output. Each cognitive function is said to operate in its own domain. For example, language is one type of cognitive function. It comprises processes specific to language, such as naming, reading and writing, and has language based rules such as grammar and syntax. Language processes information into words, stories, narratives, speech and other forms of communication that are specific to the domain of language.

The overall term for processing information of any kind is cognition. Cognitive operations fall into separate domains. Typical domain categories include attention, language, memory, intelligence, and the motor, sensory, spatial and executive functions. A neuropsychological examination of a patient will include tests developed to understand how each cognitive function operates in that individual, at that time. See Table 1 for examples.

Following this schema, we can ask ourselves if awareness, if not consciousness, can be thought of as a cognitive function and similarly analyzed by functions and output.

In the next few pages I go into detail about the clinical cases in which awareness of a cognitive function, and the operation of that function, become disconnected after an injury. Careful investigation revealed that the phenomena can occur in most cognitive domains. Let me repeat that. A brain injury can cause a disruption in awareness in one restricted area of function, leaving all other functions operating normally. The loss of awareness in a small area of function is surprisingly common after focal brain injury such as a stroke.

Schacter, McAndrews and Moscovitch (1988) surveyed a range of clinical neuropsychological syndromes in which function was intact while awareness of the function was abolished. They found that the division between function and

Table 1 Cognitive Functions

Domain	Operations	Tests	Output
Language	Name, speak, read, write	Name pictures, read text, compose text	Words, narrative, lists, complex communication
Memory	Encode, retain information	Recall, recognition, in visual and verbal modes	Retrieval of stored information
Spatial	Organize visual information into meaningful arrays	Drawing, map reading, puzzle assembly	Maps, faces, locations, spatial relationships
Attention	Maintain auditory and visual input; focus and switch at will	Follow trails, retain auditory sequences	Sustained ability to process information
Motor	complex and meaningful motor operations	Finger tapping, grip strength, meaningful gestures and skilled movement (praxis)	Timed and skilled motor activity
Executive	Categorize, sequence, initiate and inhibit behaviours	Organizing, planning, sorting, start and stop	Developing and implementing complex behaviours
Intelligence	Integrate information to achieve goal	Verbal and visual puzzles	Solutions to problems

awareness had already been documented or suggested in virtually all cognitive domains, including vision, memory, reading and language. The authors developed a model of cognitive function with the name DICE: Dissociable Interactions in Conscious Experience.

A significant idea developed in their paper was that awareness was a separate cognitive function, and not the omniscient observer we experience. Awareness, just like other cognitive functions, could be affected by a brain lesion. The effect of altered awareness could be restricted to just one aspect of one cognitive function. The authors characterized the phenomena of function without awareness as a dissociation between explicit (conscious) and implicit (unconscious) knowledge. Explicit knowledge is the knowledge that subjects are aware they possess. Implicit knowledge is expressed in performance without the subjects' awareness that they possess that very knowledge. Explicit is what you can verbalize. Implicit is what you can demonstrate.

Taking these examples together, Schacter and colleagues identified a number of common characteristics in dissociations between implicit and explicit knowledge. One aspect was the need to use indirect methods to assess for the retained but unaware, or implicit, knowledge. Simply asking a patient to do something they for which they had no conscious knowledge did not progress very far. Instead, a patient might be asked to carry out different tasks in the direct and indirect conditions.

If they were able to demonstrate knowledge or skill indirectly only, the result would be behavioural evidence of retained knowledge but lost awareness. Comparing the results of implicit and explicit test performance meant that a subjective experience could be measured. If the results of implicit testing were superior to explicit testing, there was a way to measure the absence of awareness.

One example of this method is acquired memory disorders. Amnesia is a condition in which, due to illness or injury affecting the brain, a patient is unable to recall memories, or to learn new information. A full blown amnesic syndrome usually arises from injuries to the medial temporal lobes or the middle region of the cerebral hemispheres, the diencephalon. In memory tests, patients with amnesic disorders were asked to think back and recall a recent event. They tended to do poorly when they tried consciously to remember the recent event. With less direct tasks of cued recall or recognition, the patients' performance revealed implicit (unconscious) memory for the event. The information about the event was still in memory, although the patients no longer had conscious access.

In another example, motor memory for new skills such as writing backward, or following a path on paper with a pencil using only a mirror as a guide, was retained although the subject did not recall ever learning these skills before. After seeing a list of words, amnesic patients were not able to explicitly recall which words they just saw. However, when presented with cues of a single letter, they could provide many of the words to which they had just been exposed. The memory was demonstrably there, but they were not aware of the memory and could not directly access it. The result is robust; it has been replicated with different experimental paradigms and different patients.

Schacter et al (1988) described a study in which a densely amnesic patient was taught to write computer code, edit computer programs, and use disk storage and retrieval operations. At the beginning of each session the patient claimed he had never worked on a computer before. Nonetheless, he was able to implicitly use knowledge and a range of skills that he had acquired over multiple learning sessions.

Another finding from this paper was that the disconnection between function and awareness, between implicit and explicit knowledge, occurred in a number different cognitive domains.

Consider memory for familiar faces, such as family, co-workers and friends. The neuropsychological disorder of prosopagnosia is an inability to recognize the faces of people that were once well known and familiar. This type of memory disorder can arise after lesions, or injury, to the occipital-parietal cortex. Prosopagnosia, or face blindness, can also be present from birth. In these cases, the person fails to explicitly recognize familiar faces. However, indirect testing methods show the memory is not lost; only the awareness of the knowledge is gone. One method to test for the retained ability to recognize familiar faces is to use sensors placed on the skin to record electrodermal conductivity. In healthy, unaffected persons, the skin conductance response mirrors normal recognition of familiar faces. Patients with prosopagnosia may report no recognition of familiar faces, but can show normal skin conductance reactions to familiar faces. When prosopagnosic patients were asked to learn pairs of faces and names, they were quicker to learn the familiar, properly matched pairs than the mismatched pairs. The researchers concluded that implicit memory for familiar faces had a positive effect on their ability to perform the task.

Schacter and colleagues (1988) reviewed an extensive literature on the loss of awareness in a number of cognitive functions, including the specialized task of reading. They described the results as controversial and limited, but tantalizing. The task of reading is made up of a number of different components, including letter recognition, word recognition, memory for the sounds of letters and words. Some words, such as familiar trade names and logos, can be learned as shapes. Think of the Nike 'swoosh' emblem, or the trademark Coca Cola script, as examples. There is a specific dyslexic disorder called alexia (inability to read) without agraphia (inability to write). Some of these patients did not recognize words; they have to sound the word out in a letter by letter fashion. In this way they are able to access the knowledge they still had of the word. The knowledge of words was not lost; only the conscious access to them.

Language is a very complex cognitive function. The general term for any acquired loss of language function, such as following a stroke, is aphasia. Examination of an aphasic patient involves checking speech fluency and word production; word comprehension and sentence comprehension; repetition of words and sentences; reading words and sentences; writing words and sentences. Regular words sound the way they are written ("cat") and irregular words do not sound the way they are written ("yacht"), but conscious access to just the irregular words alone can be lost after injury. As is the case with reading, stroke patients can show dissociations between awareness of their ability to use language and the actual use of language. In this review, there were examples of dissociations between awareness and function in language, speech and reading.

The authors described more examples of explicit/implicit dissociations in the DICE model. For example, the disorder of agnosia refers in general to a loss of knowledge. Visual agnosia refers to the loss of ability to identify an object by visual inspection alone. When a patient with visual agnosia is able to hold and feel the object in question, they are often able to retrieve the name correctly. They are using alternate means to retrieve the name when vision alone will no longer serve the purpose. In one case study of a patient with visual agnosia, the patient was able to name only three out of 24 pictures of common objects. When asked to decide if the picture was of an animate or inanimate object, that is, take an alternate mental route to the goal, the patient produced a correct answer in 22/24 cases.

The ability to attend, to focus and pay attention, is compromised in a syndrome called neglect, or more precisely, hemineglect. The affected patient does not attend to the space on the side opposite to the side of the brain where the stroke occurred. They are no longer aware of one half of their environment. The syndrome can interfere with the patient's capacity to look, hear, sense touch or perform a motor function. The syndrome is best known in the case when the lesion occurs in the right hemisphere of the brain, and the inattention occurs on the patient's left side. These patients may not eat food on the left side of their plate, shave the left side of their face, or in one of my patients, apply eye makeup to the left eye. Depending on the type and degree of neglect involved, they may, when asked to extend both arms, raise only one arm in the air. They may fail to notice or identify touch to the affected body side. They may not report sound in one ear. When asked to draw, they may draw one half of a clock, cat or flower. When presented with a series of lines on a page and asked to draw a line bisecting each one, their bisection lines will not fall in the middle of the line, but will be shifted to the right end.

Schacter and colleagues (1988) described some cases in which it appeared the patients who were diagnosed with neglect still had some implicit, or retained, awareness in the affected area. In one study, patients were shown one picture in the left visual field, and another one in the right visual field. They were asked to decide if the pictures were the same or different. All of the patients reported little to no sense of anything at all in the left visual field, but when asked to guess, all performed the same/different task with a high degree of accuracy. They showed implicit knowledge of the picture in the neglected field, but were unaware of the knowledge they used to perform the task.

The studies of the split brain patients is full of remarkable studies of lost awareness and retained abilities. Briefly, in the 1950's a surgical intervention for severe, intractable seizures was developed that involved severing the largest nerve bundles that connect the left and right hemispheres of the brain. (Sperry, 1977). The surgery was helpful in reducing seizure activity but also provided a unique opportunity to study the functions of each of the two hemispheres separately.

In these cases the patient's left hemisphere, typically the verbal part of the brain, is surgically disconnected from the right hemisphere, typically the nonverbal part. The verbal hemisphere no longer has access to information from the nonverbal hemisphere. However, both hemispheres are still active doing things. The verbal hemisphere is now working without all of its usual flow of information, but it will nonetheless generate a narrative to fill in the gaps. This story telling facility is so strong, and apparently hardwired, that it has been called the Interpreter (Gazzaniga, 1988). The left hemisphere of the brain specializes in telling stories, weaving together bits and pieces of information, whether accurate or not. In such a case the normal flow of information from the right hemisphere is missing and the left hemisphere keeps talking, apparently quite unaware of it.

The studies unfold in a series of research papers published in the 1960s. Two neurosurgeons, Dr. Philip Vogel and Dr. Joseph Bogen, performed surgery on a series of patients with severe and intractable seizure disorders (Sperry, 1977). The central nerve bundle connecting the left and right hemispheres of the brain was severed, in a procedure called a commissurotomy. The specific tracts severed were the corpus callosum and the anterior callosal bundle. Other, smaller bundles of fibres connecting the left and right hemispheres were left intact. This surgery was successful in that it helped reduce the number and severity of seizures, but the patients were left with two cerebral hemispheres that were functioning, for the most part, independently. The surgery permitted investigation of the functions of each, now separated, hemisphere. Dr. Michael Gazzaniga and Dr. Roger Sperry, along with the two neurosurgeons, produced a series of papers on the effects of commissurotomy on the cognitive functions of the patients.

The surgical procedure interfered with many points of communication between the hemispheres. Visual information and speech no longer crossed between hemispheres. Each hemisphere still had motor control of the contralateral hand. In those patients that had the typical organization of left hemisphere dominance for language, the left hemisphere had the capacity of speech; the right hemisphere was mute. The assumption had been, up to that point, that the right hemisphere was lacking in speech and therefore many other cognitive processes, but this new line of research demonstrated otherwise.

Frequently, the left hemisphere manages language function and so it is described as dominant for that function. The left hemisphere also controls the motor and sensory functions of the right hand. The right hemisphere typically manages spatial based skills and may be dominant for some functions such as location in space. These studies used specific techniques such that visual information was transmitted only to one hemisphere, but not to the other. The investigators could then look at what each hemisphere, in isolation, did with information.

The studies found that the right hemisphere could manage some basic language functions, such as simple spelling, reading and comprehension of speech. The right hemisphere still controlled movement on the left side of the body, because the linkages between right hemisphere and motor control of the left side of the body were not affected by the surgery. Similarly, the left hemisphere still controlled motor function on the right side of the body. This meant that after surgery, literally, the right hand did not know what the left hand was doing. This gave the researchers a remarkable opportunity to study what cognitive functions were operating in each hemisphere. The prevailing opinion had been, since the right hemisphere did not have language to express itself, that it was not very bright. Studies with these patients proved that wrong. The retained cognitive abilities of the right hemisphere, even with minimal language function, came as a surprise (Gazzaniga, 1988).

These studies showed that, even though the right hemisphere does not usually communicate in language, it is fully aware and understands what is going on around it. The left hemisphere processes everything it sees and hears with language into a linear sequence, and creates a story told in language. It will build a narrative to account for observed behaviour, even when it does not know why that behaviour occurred. Remember, in these cases, the left hemisphere has no access to what the right hemisphere knows. For example, the left hand, controlled by the mute right hemisphere, points to a series of pictures. The left hemisphere sees what the left hand its doing. It generates an explanation, a story, to account for what it saw but did not know. The experiment is repeated, with similar results. The left hemisphere consistently constructs stories and explanations with whatever information it has.

I think it is important to note that the left hemisphere does not weigh and consider the evidence before it. It does not decide there is enough information to proceed, nor does it ask questions or begin any investigation. It simply and only takes what is presented and constructs a narrative. In later chapters I present the argument that investigation, curiosity and exploration are activities of the conscious mind. The separated left hemisphere, in these studies, does not initiate those tasks.

Another interesting finding was that the individual's sense of personal identity and self awareness was not affected by the surgery (Sperry, 1977). Each hemisphere knew who "they" were. In addition, the attentional system, the process by which attention is focussed and resources allocated, was not relegated to one hemisphere or another (Gazzaniga, 1998). Attention and awareness were unaffected by surgical separation of the two major bundles of connecting tissue; they remained intact as single cognitive entities.

One might have assumed that the cerebral hemispheres were the important mediators of these functions, and that severing the connections might somehow alter them. The remaining connecting brain structures which were not separated by surgery include a number of smaller commissures between the hemispheres, as well as the cerebellum. The cerebellum is a smaller single structure which sits at the back and bottom of the left and right cerebral hemispheres. It was thought for many years that it was largely involved in motor control and coordination, but studies have emerged in recent decades of the role of the cerebellum in a range of cognitive activities. So, there are still gaps in our understanding of what brain structures are involved in which cognitive functions and at what level.

There are other ways in which awareness can unexpectedly break down, and the picture just gets more complicated.

There is a type of unexpected retained awareness where none is expected in the case of phantom pain, or retained sensory awareness of position, pain or itching, in a part of the body that has been amputated. In these cases, the patient has retained awareness although the function is gone. The retained sensation of a limb after amputation is known as phantom limb. Ramachandran and Blakeslee (1998) describe the phenomena at length, citing records going back to the sixteenth century. Following amputation, in these cases, the patient may continue to feel the presence of the limb. The sensation may resolve or persist, and can change in quality to itching, discomfort or pain. Ramachandran and Blakeslee wrote that one explanation was that the brain had a map of the body, including the now missing part, and that the brain map persisted without change after amputation.

There is another type of unexpected but apparent retained awareness, and that is in the signs of awareness in comatose patients. In Adrian Owen's *Into the Gray Zone* (2017), signs of awareness were demonstrated in persons who were in vegetative or comatose states, who were not responsive to voice and who could not show motor responses to language. There were no behavioural indications whatsoever in these patients of alertness or arousal. However, images of brain activity in real time during functional neuroimaging indicated the apparently intact capacity to signal yes or no responses to questions posed verbally to the patient. Owen wrote that there are signs of preserved awareness during what appears to be a state of unconsciousness in a proportion of all the comatose patients that he has scanned. Using functional neuroimaging, the brain scans of some of these individuals indicated responsiveness to verbal questions. The responses demonstrated awareness of events occurring around them, awareness of the passage of time, and reports of their own experiences of pain or comfort.

These comatose patients appeared to demonstrate retained awareness and comprehension of at least one form of sensory stimulus, hearing.

The cases described by Owen (2017) suggest that awareness, at least in one sensory channel, can persist in the absence of consciousness. It is not clear if the cases of phantom pain represent an alteration in what we think of as awareness. The patient with phantom pain does not see the missing limb, only feel it. The sensory experience remains in awareness when all other function is gone. In the case of stroke, awareness for just one function can be lost. The split brain studies indicated a loss of access to information, but also no curiosity about the absence of information, when each hemisphere operated in isolation.

Each of these conditions illuminates a different way in which awareness can change. What we can surmise is that these syndromes present clinically as a change in access to knowledge, such as when memory for faces is still active but can not be accessed. Let us consider what it means to access information. One element is that the affected person can no longer focus attention on the topic in question. The patient can not pay attention to the left side of the space around them. They are unable to focus on what words belong to the category of inanimate objects, or the memory of yesterday's computer training. Loss of awareness can also be stated as an inability to focus attention on a specific function. In this view, awareness is a brain function that uses attention in order to access or process information.

This chapter reviewed cognitive functions that are used consciously, as in neuropsychological assessment. The next section looks at the unconscious aspects of information processing. Do we merely store learning and experience on a shelf, or is there more processing? One way to understand any unconscious cognitive processing is to evaluate the changes that information undergoes, between learning and memory. Cognition provides an accessible pathway. Neuropsychological assessment of cognitive functions allows us to compare what comes out to what went in an accessible pathway to unconscious activities..

SECTION 2
THE LIBRARY

Chapter 3: Unconscious Cognitive Processes

THIS SECTION reviews some ideas about cognitive processes that occur outside of awareness. We presume the processes exist because sometimes information changes between leaving and re entering consciousness. The accuracy of information retention, and the types of changes that occur, are clues to these processes.

Forty years ago there was little to no information about unconscious cognitive processes. The unconscious was considered a psychiatric concept, a repository of emotion and impulse. Nisbett and Wilson (1977) published a paper that spoke to how very little access the conscious mind had to the factors that affected a person's thoughts and behaviour. Subjective reports on the reasons for a person's behaviour showed "...little or no introspective access to higher order cognitive processes" (p.104). The authors wrote that one can not rely on the conscious, aware mind to provide accurate, complete and reliable information on its unconscious functions. The aware mind was prone to blind spots and errors. Introspection was a poor tool for understanding mental functions. The aware mind was also not able to identify where consciousness ends and the unconscious begins. There was no conscious experience of any sudden edge or boundary where conscious awareness ends.

It was at the start of a period of modeling how the human brain might be organized, and what type of brain architecture might best account for observed cognitive functions. Computer based models were proposed. At that time, consciousness was seen as a type of temporary storage structure, while procedural memory was unconscious and not available to conscious inspection. It was thought that, since we have no conscious experience of the processing that occurs in the unconscious, and introspection had yielded nothing useful, the conscious mind did all the thinking.

That all began to change in the 1970's. Ideas about the relative scale of mental work were shifting.

In 1987 Kihlstrom published The Cognitive Unconscious, arguing that significant mental processes occurred in the unconscious mind. The paper contained several important ideas. First, events that could not be consciously remembered could still influence mental functions. Second, perceptual-cognitive and motor skills became routinized through repetition and mastery. At that point they became unconscious and no longer available to conscious inspection. Third, the scale of unconscious cognitive operations was much greater than could be appreciated by introspection alone. Kihlstrom's paper suggested that a great deal of cognitive work, such as the processing of experiences, thoughts and skills, occurred outside of awareness. Some of these processes were thought to be innate, such as language and visual processing, and some acquired, such as playing a piano, sports or typing. The unconscious processes functioned automatically, as they consumed no (conscious) effort or attentional resources. They could be triggered or used with the correct environmental stimuli, such as typing, and not compete with conscious, intentional activities such as talking.

Kihlstrom concluded that the functions of perception, memory, discriminative responses to stimuli, and higher processes such as judgment and problem solving were not conscious functions. "Rather, consciousness", he wrote, "is an experiential quality that may accompany any of these functions" (p. 1450).

Yet, both conscious and unconscious mental processes coexist within the same skull. Bargh (2017) reported that neuroimaging studies showed that both conscious and unconscious mental processes use the same brain region; they rely on the same geography, the same substrate, to carry out their operations. "We have a single, unified mind that operates in both conscious and unconscious modes, always using the same set of basic machinery" (p. 13).

Bargh and Morsella (2008) reviewed and re-considered theories of the structure of the unconscious in their paper, The Unconscious Mind. They returned to the earliest formulations of the unconscious. A reconsideration of theoretical approaches suggested an alternative description, in which the unconscious operated a complex and intelligent level of cognition.

The authors further argued that there are multiple, independent unconscious systems that guide behaviour. These processes involved perception, evaluation and motivation, and operated entirely outside of awareness. Take as example the various possible motor responses to the stimulus of a hammer. All are available to the unconscious mind, and are evaluated for usefulness and appropriateness given the context in which the hammer is presented. Ultimately, one use for the hammer is selected; the conscious mind becomes aware of the choice after the process is complete and the motor act is being launched.

Bargh (2017) made a clear distinction between structure and function in the brain. There was no such thing as one cerebral location for consciousness, and another for the unconscious. The modes in which cognitive function operated were not contiguous with the structures of the physical brain. Numerous activities can operate both in aware and unconscious modalities, shifting back and forth. Learning was frequently conscious, even deliberate; later use of what was learned was frequently outside of awareness. While in theory the processing of emotional content occupied both the aware and unconscious minds, research suggested that processing of cognitive and social content also occurred in both modalities. There appear to be innate, and unconscious, processes for forming social bonds, acting cooperatively and developing social groups.

Bargh concluded that the unconscious never sleeps and never rests. This meant the contents of the unconscious were constantly available to influence behaviour, and therefore, "The past is always present". The influence of the unconscious on current behaviour was informed by all previous experience.

Consciously acquired skills, attitudes and assumptions became the unconscious means to process information quickly without expending awareness resources. These recent acquisitions became rules to live by and working assumptions. Bargh characterized them as adaptive unconscious mechanisms. He described the process by which such an unconscious mechanism was developed as "conscious-first". Initially the skill or process was learned with intention and conscious attention paid at each step. With enough practice the skill became streamlined and efficient. Once automated the skill or process dropped out of awareness.

The work with split brain patients provided significant clues to that process. Bargh wrote that when he began graduate studies in the mid seventies, cognitive psychology had determined that there were "...hidden, underlying mechanisms that guided or even created our thoughts and actions". The way those mechanisms operated was still unclear, but a major breakthrough in the late 1970's came from the work of Michael Gazzaniga, who had argued that not only did the unconscious mind generate behaviour, but that the conscious mind made up a plausible, but not always true, story after the fact to account for the behaviour which the unconscious had generated.

Bargh (2017) was in agreement with Kihlstrom (1987) in that they both concluded the conscious mind had a much smaller role in mental processes than originally thought.

Bargh (2017) expressed another important idea when he argued that one of the chief mechanisms by which the unconscious retains information is by developing and refining categories. The unconscious creates a system for the storage of new experiences and information.

A case in point is found in studies in dyslexia, the acquired loss of a language function. Humans acquire language according to a complex set of rules which are thought to be innate. As we learn words, they are organized by categories. The categories can include, for example, whether a word is a real word (apple) or a non word (mant), or whether the word represents a category of food (fruit) or object (furniture). Written words can be categorized in the brain by shape (orthographics), such as the shape of the logo of a famous product, or meaningfulness. Written words can be categorized by whether a word sounds like it is written (cat) or whether is pronounced differently from the way it is written (yacht). There are separate categories for words which represent animate and inanimate things; different coloured things; things starting with different letters; names typically reserved for male or female persons; and so forth. All of these categories have been identified in studies of persons who have experienced a stroke and subsequently lost access to one category or another.

All new words are analyzed and filed into categories based on their attributes. Bargh concluded it is the same with new things and new people. Bargh identified a number of categories in which we place new things or people. There is a category for me and not-me; a category for us and not-us; and a host of categories for language, culture, skill, and so forth. Each new person we meet is allocated a place in each category, and the sum describes our initial impressions of that person.

The mind constantly processes new information, events and people by identifying, sorting and categorizing. All of these processes can occur automatically, without conscious, aware mental engagement. It is also the case that such processing can be fully conscious. A botanist on a field trip, a car enthusiast, or anyone with specialized knowledge can and may consciously run through a mental checklist of attributes (Studebaker, 1957, four door, dark green) that assists with identification and memory formation.

Wilson (2002) provided a social psychology perspective on the unconscious. Social psychologists had been developing models for the way people process information about the social world, entirely outside of awareness. He characterized those models as the Adaptive Unconscious, to emphasize the active processes involved. He defined the unconscious as mental processes that are inaccessible to consciousness but that influence judgments, feelings or behaviour.

Similar to Bargh's (2017) conclusion from Gazzaniga's (1988) investigation of the "silent" right hemisphere, Wilson concluded that the unconscious is not single mind, but rather a collection of multiple modules, each devoted to a specific type of task, and each operating outside of awareness. The term "adaptive unconscious" was meant to encompass a number of disparate cognitive modules such as learning one's first language or acquiring social bonds, that developed in adaptation to environment.

Wilson also concluded that the unconscious mind influences conscious perceptions and actions by way of predictions. The predictions are based on the stored, unconscious, information about what to expect from the world and the people in it. In this model it is the role of the aware mind to respond to situations in which the prediction fails, and something unexpected or unpredicted happens. The conscious mind responds to novelty, unexpected differences and unanticipated activity.

The idea of prediction as a method to build conscious experience has had a large influence on the subsequent modeling of consciousness.

Schacter, McAndrews and Moscovitch (1988) had set up a model in which cognitive functions such as memory and language could operate on an implicit (unconscious) basis, but could also be available to the aware mind as needed. Wilson's concept of the adaptive unconscious similarly addressed the duality of some cognitive functions operating in either modality of the unconscious and the aware minds.

Wilson (2002) considered other cognitive functions, such as learning, and concluded that unconscious modules engaged in implicit learning. This type of processing occurred effortlessly and outside of awareness. In Wilson's view, implicit learning was one of the most important functions of the adaptive unconscious. He wrote that the unconscious is capable of acquiring a great deal of complex information. Additionally, the unconscious acts as a type of gatekeeper, deciding what type of information to admit back to the conscious mind. This gatekeeper function is responsible for the rapid judgments we make on other's behaviours, reading into them assumptions we make about the motives, intentions and dispositions of others. Our personal prejudices and previous determinations are contents of the unconscious. They rapidly inform our judgment about others. It is the unconscious mind that determines whether they will be present in our conscious mind and influence our actions.

The concept that the unconscious mind provides knowledge and determinations to influence the conscious mind is also seen in Bargh's (2017) work.

This process of developing agendas and selecting responses is part of a set of activities known as executive functions. Other functions that can be performed outside of awareness include goal setting, interpretation and evaluation. Wilson (2002) described it as: "The adaptive unconscious thus plays a major executive role in our mental lives. It gathers information, quickly and efficiently" (p.35). The readiness to choose a particular course of action is determined not only by personal relevance, but also by the recency of the information or category of action, and how frequently it has been encountered. "People are creatures of habit.", he wrote, "and the more they have used a particular way of judging the world, the more energized [readily activated] that concept will be" (p.37).

Wilson thereby placed executive functions alongside other automatic cognitive processes that reside in the unconscious but that can be consciously accessed or activated. This supported Schacter and colleagues' (1988) position that cognitive functions and awareness were separable, and that some cognitive functions could operate either in aware or unconscious mode.

If we become so adept at certain executive tasks, such as rapid clinical conclusions in a health care setting or determining the best course of action in an emergency, do these considerations eventually operate outside of awareness? Wilson decided the answer was yes.

In view of the number of cognitive functions that could operate outside of awareness, Wilson concluded that consciousness was a limited capacity system, reacting to external stimuli, with much information remaining outside of awareness. He then undertook a review of what is known or thought to occur in the unconscious mind as contrasted with the aware mind. He wrote that the unconscious mind has multiple systems, has an on-line pattern detector, is concerned with the here-and-now immediate, is automatic in that it is fast, unintentional, uncontrollable and effortless, is rigid and precocious (present early on) and is sensitive to negative information. A defining feature of the unconscious mind is its capacity to operate on automatic pilot.

In contrast, the conscious mind is a single system, is an after the fact check and balancer, takes the long view, is slow, intentional, controllable and effortful, is flexible, is slower to develop and is sensitive to positive information (Wilson, 2002).

Wilson argued that the two minds each develop their own habitual ways of interacting with the world, or personalities. Each has "...distinctive, characteristic ways of interpreting the social environment and stable motives that guide...behaviour" (op. cit. p.72).

The concept of unconscious cognitive processing influencing behaviour has shown explanatory power elsewhere. Pally (2005) laid out a comprehensive review of the cognitive functions of the unconscious in the context of the psychiatric process of analysis. She wrote that what is learned and conditioned in the very young mind by way of experience becomes a model of reality which influences later perception. Those percepts exist in emotional models of the way the world works. The models predict how an adult will feel about security and threat, attachment and emotional bonds. These very early and basic models of what to expect in the world persist and influence relationships and feelings in the adult.

Pally makes an important point, that it is possible to re examine the early experiences, and the assumptions they create, with conscious effort. Similar to Wilson (2002), she concluded the conscious mind can examine, alter and correct errors in unconscious content. In the psychiatric context, the self examination portion is not introspection. This process is carried out with a therapist.

This may be another defining feature separating conscious and unconscious contents. The aware mind can examine the contents of consciousness and correct errors. It may be editing a paper, reconsidering facts assumed to be true, checking calculations against a table of references.

Altering the contents of the unconscious seems to require independent assistance in the form of a second party, such as coach, guide or therapist.

In recalling early childhood events, the therapist assists with re evaluation and interpretation in the frame of adult perception. A sports coach observes an athlete's habitual way of doing something and provides feedback on which elements are not useful or optimal. Reviewing a memory of an old event with another person who was present can bring to light errors in perception or meaningfulness.

The mechanisms by which the unconscious stores information are rigid and resist change. The information itself can, with specific mechanisms involving outside parties, be altered. In these models, the information residing in the unconscious modulates or influences behaviour without necessarily emerging into consciousness.

Psychology underwent a crisis in the 20-tens when a number of social psychology studies could not be replicated. Much work on unconscious influences on behaviour came into question. I place greater weight on the split brain studies and the implicit/explicit knowledge work, and the concepts of mental processes operating unconsciously makes sense and holds up across several disciplines. Ideas about the ways in which the unconscious influences the conscious mind will undergo further debate, but in the meantime I think it is interesting to retain some convergence of ideas. In the next chapter we will consider other examples of unconscious storage and processing of information.

Chapter 4: The Library

THE PRECEDING chapters considered the roles of consciousness and awareness in information processing and management. Information is processed and transferred between conscious and unconscious modalities as part of a system that takes in raw data and ultimately influences complex behaviours. This chapter looks at ways in which information is stored in the unconscious, and ways in which information changes while in storage. The concept of unconscious information storage is referred to as the Library, for convenience.

WHEN WE look at what we can recall, or use, from this store of memories, we see that some mechanisms of learning are more durable than others, and some result in fewer errors. We may need to rely on memory, but it is hard to know with any certainty which information in storage is free of errors. We do not know entirely how unconscious memory is structured, or how information in the unconscious might be processed.

To begin, not a lot is known about the inner workings of the unconscious. It remains a black box problem. It is not accessible to introspection or direct testing (Nisbett and Wilson, 1977). It is even difficult to form a clear concept of what it does. Psychological research on the mechanics of unconscious determinants of social behaviour has experienced replication problems. In particular, studies on priming social behaviour with unconscious determinants have come under question (Diener and Biswas-Diener, 2017).

Some work on unconscious cognitive operations is well accepted. Chapter 2 presented an overview of work on unconscious cognitive processing, which suggested that there are reasons to believe that information storage and processing mechanisms are in place (Kihlstrom, 1987; Wilson, 2002). Consciously acquired information, emotions and experiences, skills, routines and habits all appear to persist outside of awareness, in a conceptual space we refer to as the unconscious (Kihlstrom, 1987; Bargh, 2017). For convenience we speak of this as information storage.

It is not entirely clear how information is organized in unconscious storage, but it is presumed that some storage mechanism is present (Bargh, 2017). In looking to model unconscious processes in information management, I relied on some assumptions. One assumption is that the ways in which things are learned most efficiently and best remembered are clues to the ways in which that information is stored. The types of information which, once acquired, recede from awareness but are later available to awareness, may be stored in ways that are similar to the ways they were learned. In this group are procedures, complex motor skills, hierarchical structures and spatial arrays.

To begin, some basics of how we learn.

Some types of information are acquired so efficiently that there are minimal errors in later recall and use. Ways in which information can be processed for optimal recall include creating pattern and narrative. For example, in cultures without written language or widespread literacy, oral history in the form of narrative, rhyming, music, chanting and dance can all, often in combination, encode information simultaneously in multiple domains. This is a powerful method to learn and retain large amounts of information (Steeves, 2021).

The more ways in which a piece of information is processed, the stronger the memory. This means that if you use multiple cognitive domains to learn something, the more likely you will be to recall it at a later time. This means involvement in a multiple step process, such as memorizing Shakespeare by watching and performing in plays, or demonstrating and carrying out an experiment in a chemistry lab.

Many years ago I watched a documentary series about an Indigenous woman from Canada who decided to visit different cultures to learn about their traditional healing practices (https://en.wiki-pedia.org/wiki/Medicine_Woman). In one episode, Dr. Daniele Biehn followed a group of indigenous women who were foraging for medicinal plants. When they discovered a useful plant in a new location, they formed a circle and generated a song, accompanied by a dance, to remember the plant and its location. They were, in effect, encoding the memory of the identity and location of the plant in multiple modalities. As a group they had a mechanism to amplify and share important information.

If one needs to memorize apparently random information, one of the most effective techniques is to build a narrative on to the data. For example, random number strings are hard to remember, but meaningful numbers are easier. One of the methods we use in neuropsychological testing is to ask the patient to recall random numbers. We start with two or three numbers, and work up to longer strings. At some point the patient will no longer be able to recite the numbers back correctly. This is a story told to me by one technician when she was trying to get the best possible performance out of an older male patient. After some frustrating attempts she finally said, "Now pay attention! I am giving you Halle Berry's phone number!". It was not standard test administration, but he did remember that number string correctly. Memory is enhanced if seemingly random information is meaningful.

Taking random pieces of data and creating a pattern will also improve memory. In graduate school, a professor was teaching a group of us students about a type of memory test involving a word list. She gave the test to us, reciting the string of fifteen random words one per second. She then instructed us to write down as many as we could recall. I had worked as a psychometrist giving tests such as this, and I knew the trick to successful recall. As she said the words, I imagined a story line using each word. When the time came to write them down, I could remember the story more easily than just a list of words by rote recall. This is the same method used in memory competitions such as remembering the sequence of one, two or three decks of cards. The random data points become images and the images are strung together as a story, and the story has a meaningful sequence that can be remembered.

Another principle of memory storage is repetition. It is an old principle of learning that repetitive linkages between stimulus and response form a neural link and this link is the basis of memory. How many times did you recite the times tables before you had them down cold? How many times did you ride (and fall off) a bike before you had the balance just right? Over learned information is so deeply encoded that later recall is very robust.

One of the most over learned pieces of information you have acquired is your name, and it is one of the most durable memories. It is one memory that survives even the most severe brain injuries. It is possible for people to forget their names, but it does not happen because of a blow to the head. The scene in which someone is struck on the head, perhaps knocked out, but later can not remember their name, is fiction. However, in rare cases, people are found wandering far from home, not knowing who they are or where they came from. These cases are felt to be related to a very significant emotional trauma underlying this level of disorientation and amnesia.

That well learned content such as skills or habits are very difficult to change, speaks to the durability of those types of memories. Conscious examination and change of some unconscious material usually requires outside help. If you want to change your golf swing or alter your emotional responses, your best hope lies with a coach or therapist to provide feedback and guidance.

If there is only one opportunity to learn something in order to remember it later, the thing is better retained if the single episode is meaningful in some fashion. Meaningful may mean that the new thing is vital to survival, or a piece of a puzzle. If a new piece of information is consistent with other things you already accept as fact, the new information is more readily retained. It is easily slotted into place in the context of other similar items. This is the case if you already have a body of knowledge on a subject; the next item that fits in that group is more easily retained.

To understand something is to improve one's chances of remembering it. Every once in a while, something is beyond our capacity to recognize and slot into any category, that it is not easily captured and filed; it disappears. For example, the story goes that the first few times the Wright brothers flew their plane, it went unremarked by the locals because it simply was beyond the current understanding of things that fly in the sky. In those days, nothing flew in the sky but birds. In another example, consider learning something new, like how to distinguish bird calls. If you have no knowledge of the distinct calls of different birds, you will not easily remark on the variety of birds you hear. If there is no fund of knowledge for bird calls already in place in your unconscious, you will have difficulty efficiently distinguishing and remembering bird calls. You will need to consciously build up data points in that category before you can become proficient in discerning new ones.

It is also the case that a strong emotional overlay is associated with a durable memory. The flashbulb moment is a clear and durable memory of the moment in time in which you learned of a major public event. The first landing on the moon, the assassination of John F. Kennedy and the attack on the World Trade Towers in New York are considered flashbulb memories for many. This is also the case with the category Schacter (1999) refers to as persistent, even intrusive, memories that one might prefer to forget. The disorder of post traumatic stress is an example of strong emotional overlay linked to intrusive memory.

Finally, consider visual memory. A jumble of random lines or colours are just like random words:

hard to remember. A set of streets and alleys in a strange city can be disorienting. Once you see a pattern in the colours or lines, or build a mental map of the city with some landmarks to pin it all down, you have a meaningful pattern to remember. The same principle holds for notes and music.

While there are multiple mechanisms to enhance storage for later recall, some types of memory are more accurate than others. Procedures, such as riding a bike or operating machinery, return to awareness in their entirety, step after step. This type of memory retrieval is accurate, as long as one does not interfere with the running of the program by thinking too much about it. Recognition memory, for something previously learned such as a place or face, is also quick and accurate if not overthought. It is a relatively quick task for the mind to compare new stimuli to stored memory to determine if there is a match. In contrast, memory for events is remarkably inaccurate and error prone. This type of recall is based on a process of reassembling elements into a narrative that is believed to be true. Eye witness accounts may be accepted in courts, but research has documented their low reliability.

Transferring information from consciousness to storage in the unconscious ranges from automatic to effortful, from accurate to error prone. This continuum of effort might have implications for the structure and purpose of unconscious mechanisms.

If we order the types of memory along a continuum, from durable to fragile, the strongest memories are over learned items like our names; flashbulb moments; the things that threaten survival and social self ("I never forgot that lesson") and the physical realities of the world. This information informs the prediction function, which we rely upon to build a set of accurate expectations of the world. If something goes to memory automatically, is accurate and is forever after accessible, I would argue it is of higher priority than something that requires much more effort, repetition, multimodal processing and other devices such as are used to learn playing card sequences. I think this speaks to where the unconscious mind preferentially devotes its resources.

The continuums of automatic to effortful, accurate to error prone, suggests that there are different types of storage in the unconscious. In this hypothetical library, many categories and types of information are stored, but not all are accessed in the same manner. Some material, on which survival depends, may be accessed with urgency. Material that is used every day is called upon frequently. Some material is used in considering an ongoing problem and is more readily available. Not everything is organized in the same fashion. Faces and locations are specific visual arrays, and can be sorted according to familiarity, importance and frequency of use. This library does not use the Dewey decimal system.

The concept of memory as a library implies passive storage. It may be more helpful to include the concepts of an archive, which is not accessible to a conscious search, and the stacks, which can be scanned at will. There are ways to provide unconscious information to the conscious mind automatically, as a situation requires. There appears to be a system that responds to questions, especially repeated or heartfelt questions. This is suggested by the experience of Poincaré as described by Sacks (2017). After pondering a mathematics problem for months without success, Poincaré had a sudden insight to the answer, fully formed and complete. There was no new information in the answer that came to him; it was a rearrangement of information he already knew. This is the experience of things suddenly falling into place. It is a stock item in any mystery novel.

To return to the library metaphor, let us say at birth there is a basic organizational system, with manuals on basic behaviours already in the archive. The stacks are largely empty. The first material acquired is experiential: temperature, hunger, attachment. It is not easily catalogued, but some argue that all experience is retained and everything has to go on a shelf somewhere in the stacks. As time goes by and information accumulates, experience allows for greater complexity in the storage system. The individual takes what the world has to offer in the way of experience and information and builds systems to retain it. The ways in which we learn information breaks down by type of information. The ways in which information is used in or out of consciousness, the ease of conscious access, and the amount of error, reflects not just storage but priority access to resources. Some memories are not as well protected as others.

The presumed functions in an information storage system could include information acquisition, organizing, retrieval and recirculation.

In terms of information acquisition, the process starts right after birth. The earliest experiences are a mixture of passive reception of events outside of control, and attempts to actively figure out how to achieve some goals, such as attention, food and warmth. Some of the earliest library volumes might be Howling and Crying 101, Cute and Smiling, Throwing Toys Out of the Pram and Grab That Thing.

One important goal, from birth onwards, is to populate the mental library with information about the world that is necessary for survival. To that end the conscious mind is curious and exploring. It practices movement, develops skills, makes determinations and judgments, comes to conclusions, builds an explanatory narrative. It considers, weighs and organizes. At some point the processing of some particular thing concludes, and the resulting content leaves awareness and becomes unconscious. This content might end up in the archive as a volume titled, Living Hand to Mouth: The Basics of Self Feeding.

The young conscious mind is like the business end of a vacuum cleaner, pulling up everything in its path. From the very first step, in which the vacuum mouth is directed in one direction or another, organization is imposed on the data stream.

Building content for the library, the unconscious mind, means organizing information in such a way that it can be used or consciously recalled. Consider how we learn. Information is better learned when it is meaningful. Meaningfulness is a term reflecting context and emotional content. Something might be meaningful because it s consistent with emotional schema already in place, or it elicits strong primal emotions such as pleasure or fear. Pleasure is an emotional response and can be an element in visual memory, as in a visual array that is pleasing due to regularity, colour, form or pattern. Patterns are innately pleasing, and anything which can be made into a regular pattern is easier to learn. Stories are the pattern form for language. Consider a grid pattern for cities or the use of landmarks. Music is a complex of pleasant and familiar patterns of rhythm and tones which, when associated with something, can make it easier to remember. Recall the story of the foraging women who marked the location of a special plant with singing and dancing specific to that item in that place. Repetition enhances many forms of memory, including motor skills. Information is learned in all these ways. All methods impart pattern, which makes learning more efficient.

Meaning is a form of context or emotional valence that enhances learning. It can take many forms. Something can be meaningful if it makes sense, in light of what else you know. Meaningfulness can take the form of satisfaction: 'I feel like I have accomplished something meaningful". It can be an interpretation of events: "Do you know what this means to me?" It can be a pivotal fact that binds elements together into something whole: "This changes everything". I remember what happened on June 10, 2016 because it was my first day on a new job and there was a flood in the offices. We were forced to work in temporary quarters down the hall.

Meaning is so important to forming new memories and knowledge that it can become a goal all on its own: the search for meaning or the wish to lead a meaningful life. Meaning makes high quality, durable content for the library.

Information is retrieved from memory for a variety of reasons. One used every day, all day is the ability to predict the external world. Knowing what to expect next, and what you can rely on, is based on the knowledge held in the library. The more information, the more elaborate the prediction model. A well stocked library provides the background information by which we understand what we experience. It allows us to respond to what we believe to be important and set the rest aside. As the unconscious knowledge base, the contents of the library, increases, an individual's capacity to respond quickly and efficiently to the environment increases.

Aside from prediction, there are other avenues to retrieve information. These include a need to know avenue, methods for correcting errors, methods to rehearse and refine and a method to query information and ask questions. Quick, automatic and accurate retrieval reflects a higher priority, whereas retrieval that is slow, effortful and full of errors reflects a lower priority function.

The idea is that, in a system of finite resources, there will be priorities for attention, effort and resources. If your brain is largely preoccupied with other matters, paying attention to where you left the car keys may not be its highest priority. Preoccupation, the condition where the limited resource of attention is already engaged, is the source of many errors in learning and recall. Multi tasking does not actually mean doing more at the same time, it means doing more with less attention on each task. Attention is limited; awareness is finite; resources are allocated by need.

Let us look at the continuum of speed. Which memories arrive in consciousness the quickest? I would assume it is the function we never notice, which is prediction. If you are conscious, prediction is active. You know where you are and who you are. This is a higher priority retrieval. You need to know where you are more than you need to know what your grandmother's dining room looked like. As-needed retrieval is the basis of, for example, fast thinking in Kahneman's Thinking Fast and Slow (2011) paradigm. We are able to make rapid decisions and act quickly when necessary because there is a mental priority for that type of response.

The external environment provides many cues for as needed retrieval of memory and information to the conscious mind. A familiar face approaches you, and you need the name and why you know that person quickly. The name and relationship comes to mind. You sit down in your car and need to get underway; the motor programs for turning key, putting on seatbelt, checking mirror all line up and execute automatically. You read a manuscript, pen in hand, and need the correct spelling of a word such as "accommodate". All may be provided briskly by the unconscious library.

The internal conscious landscape is constantly dipping into the library. ("She mentioned learning the times table, what is 6x7?"; "I meant to call my boss this afternoon, what points did I want to cover?" "Did Sam take his lunch to school this morning, and did I feed the cat?")

There is a category of stored information which the conscious mind can not intentionally and consciously access. In McGilchrist's (2019) formulation, it is less The Master and more The Emissary. It is largely autonomous and not very responsive to one's bidding. I think of it as the archive rather than the shelves of a library. There are occasions on which you would like to check material in the library for errors. You would like to reconsider your assessment of a group of people. You want to change your running stride or golf swing. You wonder if you have misread the room. You need to relearn how to walk after an injury. Childhood trauma is affecting your adult relationships.

Self correction of unconscious library contents is possible, but it is effortful. It usually requires a mechanism for external feedback as introspection is a poor tool for accessing unconscious material (Nisbett and Wilson, 1977). A coach, a physiotherapist, a psychoanalyst all assist in achieving behavioural change through independent review, feedback and suggested correction. The process of consciously changing unconscious contents takes work; it is not automatic.

There will be material that ended up in the stacks with little or no processing. Perhaps it was the baby's experience at a very simple level. Perhaps it was something for which there were no words, or no way to understand, at the time of the experience. Perhaps it was something so very challenging or horrific that jamming it back into the stacks without any further consideration was the safest thing to do. Such things can continue to influence behaviour throughout the lifespan. Every once in a while there is a need to pull such a thing out of memory and try to reprocess it. Consciousness is capable of reconsidering the old material and providing a fresh take so that it can be properly catalogued, shelved back in the stacks and forgotten. That such a process is associated with behavioural change supports the model.

Schacter (1999) talks about the seven sins of memory, a counting of all the ways memory fails us. His work indicates that conscious access to unconscious contents is error prone. There are, however, information retrieval systems that are fast and accurate.

The fund of knowledge in the unconscious, the library and the archive, feeds a steady stream of impeccably accurate information to the prediction model (Wilson, 2002). Accurate predictions provide you with everything you count on: that a sunny sky is blue, that gravity will cause you to fall, that you will be able to see when you open your eyes. The unconscious is busy. Wondering where you left your car keys is not its top priority.

Information does not sit passively in storage. Some is circulated and reused. Information, skills, experience and knowledge circulate from the conscious mind to the unconscious, and return to the conscious mind in implicit or explicit forms. While some templates, such as the capacity to learn language, sense and control movement are inborn (Kihlstrom, 1987), the knowledge acquired in the world starts in conscious experience. The raw data of experience is altered, modified and transformed not only in conscious cognitive processing, but also in unconscious cognitive processes. There is a continuous flow of content, between the conscious and unconscious mind. Learn, store, retrieve, use and repeat.

An implication of this cycle is that there are mechanisms to perpetuate the flow. The conscious mind learns things, and that information recedes into the unconscious. The unconscious constantly provides information to the conscious mind, whether it be automatic prediction, responsive need to know or searches in response to queries. The unconscious mind has its own priorities; resources are allocated accordingly. Wilson refers to this as a gatekeeper function, determining what information will become conscious (2002).

I argued above that learning occurs in the conscious mind, but that implies intentional learning. It is only one mechanism. There is incidental learning, in which information is acquired unintentionally, while attention is focussed elsewhere. For example, you are in a room full of paintings and in conversation with someone. While, they are speaking, your eyes wander to another spot in the room. Your attention is on what the other person is saying while your eyes are focussed elsewhere. Later you may be able to recall having seen one of the paintings, but not remarking on it at the time. You did not pay attention to it at the time, but you nonetheless recorded it. Wilson (2002) concluded that the unconscious engages in learning outside of awareness, and that this level of learning is very complex.

A more active form of acquiring new information is curiosity and exploration. This is perhaps strongest in childhood (Gopnik, 2021), but it never stops. Even in those persons for whom strength, stamina or mobility limit activity, something new will arouse interest and focus. The sense of something unknown will unfailingly focus attention, if not exploration. Curiosity is such a strong and universal experience that I suspect it is an automatic drive. Curiosity drives the discovery of something not already known, and that leads to new information. I suspect that the information cycle that circulates between conscious and unconscious modes is propelled by curiosity, exploration, investigation and analysis. The processes lead to new knowledge, which recedes into unconsciousness, leaving curiosity in search of a new target.

What we see from the foregoing is that some unconscious cognitive processes are faster and more reliable than others. Motor skills are more robust than memory for events. Procedures are more reliable than word recall. This continuum of accuracy and reliability can be thought of also as a set of priorities. Mental resources are finite, and some functions are more efficient than others. The priorities become more evident in normal aging, where word finding difficulty and poor recall for recent episodic memory is normal and not considered a sign of disease. As resources decline with age, some functions are better supported than others.

Human needs, such as for social connections, food or shelter, will set up the conditions for developing new information. The conscious mind acquires new content, such as how to build better shelter, but the urge to do so is part of what Gopnik (2021) calls the Exploiter Consciousness. This is the point at which information and skills already acquired are used to achieve a goal. This can cause a cascade of new learning. Take, for example, deciding to build a better shelter. Perhaps there is knowledge already in place as to how to build a basic shelter, but the goal is to build it better. Acquiring that information might take experimenting, consulting with others, apprenticing with an established builder or taking formal instruction. The prompt this time for new learning was not curiosity, but creation. The additional learning serves a different, but still adaptive, purpose.

The store of knowledge held outside of consciousness becomes available to fuel better prediction, more curiosity and greater adaptation to the environment. The cycle is ongoing while knowledge increases.

SECTION 3
THE RING OF TRUTH

Chapter 5: The Transfer of Knowledge

The unconscious has been described as a black box because we have very limited access to its contents. Information can not be reliably and accurately extracted at will. What is available, eventually, to awareness is a mixture of qualitative and quantitative material. Dreams, sudden inspirations, solutions to problems, automatic responses, predictions, expectations all arrive in consciousness under their own steam, with their own set of priorities.

What arises spontaneously from the unconscious into awareness falls into several broad categories: memory, predictions and ideas. The unconscious function of generating prediction creates a backdrop for awareness, but the predictions sit in consciousness rather than in awareness. We are, for example, not aware of the various mirages our brain generates, such as vision in the blind spot. I do not think it would be accurate to say that the experience of vision in the blind spot is unconscious.

The first category of information coming into consciousness is memory of previously learned things.

Memory covers a lot of territory, including vocabulary, skilled motor activities like handling power tools, procedural memory such as the steps in chess gambits, episodic memory of earlier events, and so on. At the same time, some additional information hitchhikes a ride along, which is called incidental memory. Incidental learning occurs when information is added to memory, even though it was not the focus of attention.

Some memories appear on cue, such as motor skills and procedural skills. Do I remember how to operate a manual transmission or ride a bike? I'll know when I turn on the ignition, or sit on the saddle of the bike. A conscious search for information yields results, but not always without effort and not always with high accuracy. Where do I keep the household accounts, how do I set up this new piece of electronic gadgetry, when did I see that person last, what is the name of that Mediterranean soup, why does salt water freeze at a different temperature than fresh water? Let me try to remember that because I do know it.

Some information emerges into awareness as needed, as the situation dictates. If you unexpectedly meet someone you know, hopefully their name comes to mind as you greet them. Sometimes the name does not come immediately to mind, but that sort of naming failure represents not only that a system of a specific type

– on demand – exists, but that it did not work that time as it should.

Then there is the curious situation of a clear memory which turns out to be false.

One property of narrative retrieved from the unconscious is the poor correlation with fact. Oliver Sacks (2017) discusses this problem in his essay, The Fallibility of Memory (pp 101-122). False memories are not uncommon events, and feel "...vivid, detailed and concrete" (p.104). He described remembering a thermite bomb falling in the garden near his house during the World War II Blitz in 1940-41. His family corrected his recall, telling him he was not even present when the bomb fell. He felt astounded. The memory was real to him. He had apparently taken his brother's account of the event and mentally constructed his own memory.

Unconscious processes appear to be able to manufacture complex, realistic, compelling memories of things that never happened. The strong sense of truth associated with such memories is a clue as to how the unconscious processes information.

In Sacks' (2017) view, the unconscious contents, such as information held in memory, were not a disorganized jumble of material. In order to be truly useful, the contents of memory must be meaningful. Lacking this quality, memory is mechanistic, like a copying machine (p.136). In the instance of his memory of the thermite bomb, the meaning was the threat to his family and home.

In addition to the problem of false memory is the problem of faulty memory. Schacter (1999) discusses at length the ways in which memory does not serve. He identified seven ways in which memory can and will fail. He named the types of failure transience, absent mindedness, blocking, misattribution, suggestibility, bias and persistence.

Transience refers to forgetting over time. Absent mindedness refers to lapses of attention when encoding into memory, and subsequent failure of memory. Blocking is a temporary failure to retrieve previously learned information, even with cueing. Tip of the tongue experience, and interfering, intrusive errors occur in blocking. The frequency of intrusion errors increases with age. Misattribution is remembering the source of the memory incorrectly, as well as attributing the source to oneself rather than an external source. Misattribution is also the memory of something that never happened. The confidence for the false memory can be as high as for accurate recall. Sometimes the error is in the correct category, reflecting a 'gist' type error.

Schacter (1999) writes that suggestibility is the incorporation of information from others into memories. Information supplied at the time of memory retrieval can lead to the creation of false memories in autobiographical information. Bias occurs because "memory encoding and retrieval are highly

dependent on, and influenced by, preexisting knowledge and beliefs." (p. 193). "People's recollections
tend to exaggerate the consistency between their
past and present attitudes, beliefs, and feelings."
(op.cit.) Persistence: "...involves remembering a fact
or event that one would prefer to forget." (p. 195).
These are repetitive and intrusive memories.

Schacter (1999) views these types of failures as
by-products of otherwise adaptive systems. For
example, disposing of unnecessary information;
suppressing recall when it would be intrusive or
unnecessary; a reduction of overly rich and unnecessary detail; not encoding the source of information when such detail might be excessive to need
or storage capacity. Even though bias may creep
in, the influence of pre existing schema is actually
helpful in organizing information. Finally, persistence of negative events might be adaptive in
learning what to avoid in the future.

There are some types of memory lapses in which
insufficient attention was paid in the learning
phase, due to problems such as absent mindedness,
misattribution and suggestibility. These failings
are all related to problems at the encoding end.
This leaves four types of errors occurring outside
of attention and we can consider whether these
imply structure at the unconscious level. These
are transience, which is forgetting over time due
to a lack of rehearsal; blocking, a retrieval problem
(including 'gist' errors); bias, reflecting the effects
of earlier learning and persistence, the unwilled
leakage of high intensity memory.

Transience is a phenomenom of episodic memory. Episodic memory means recalling an event. The process involves reassembling of elements into a memory. The process is prone to error. Such vulnerability suggests that this type of memory may not be a high priority for long term storage. Episodic memory will wane over time unless rehearsed and refreshed. Perhaps episodic memory has a higher mental priority in the early stages. It is probably the kind of memory that is most often involved in conscious acts of creation and constructing. Contemporaneous notes, those that are created within a short period of time after the event, are far more reliable that notes from a later point in time. A court of law may give greater credence to daily journal entries as a valid depiction of facts than to recall at any later time. In Ontario, the regulatory authorities hold that medical charting should be done as early as possible after seeing a patient. If episodic memory is documented long after the event occurred, information in the intervening period of time can cause distortions in recall.

Blocking, a type of retrieval error, also suggests that a conscious desire to remember something is not a high priority for the unconscious. Conscious recollection is an effortful route and not an automatic route in the way that sitting on a bicycle immediately supplies the knowledge of how to ride.

Bias errors show that information is stored in the context of personal experience, skill and knowledge.

Persistence reflects the storage of information with a strong emotional content. It demonstrates the role of the amygdala, an emotion processing structure in the brain which lies alongside the hippocampus. The hippocampus is a structure crucial in the formation of episodic memory.

So, memory errors reflect key elements of the knowledge system: attention, conscious processing, the role of meaning in the formation of memory and the priorities of the unconscious memory store. There appears to be a gradient of stability for information stored in memory. The gradient may reflect priorities. Prediction is a high priority function, but responding quickly and accurately to conscious requests for information is not.

Not all information is stored the same way in the unconscious library. The ways in which information is encoded reflect specific principles. These principles include meaning, similarity, repetition at point of acquisition and repetition in terms of frequency of use. The accuracy, speed and reliability of the recall processes suggest that some information has a higher priority and may also reflect the sheer volume of information a curious and exploratory being might amass in their lifetime.

Sacks (2017) noted that the constructed memory was subjectively indistinguishable from memories that others could validate. This is the nature of episodic memory, the recall or reassembly of events at a later time. It is not unlike the story concocted by the left hemisphere Interpreter described by Gazzaniga (1988). Accuracy is not the point or goal of this unconscious process; constructing a plausible narrative is the point. This suggests something very important about unconscious processing of information: a meaningful pattern may be a higher priority than accuracy.

Other ways in which the capacity to shift information into novel configurations is useful is in the conscious attempt to correct previous learning. These can be errors in the original memory, or clumsy motor skills that need improvement, or misunderstandings between people. Unconscious information can be altered by conscious intent.

Probably the single most resource intensive information system is prediction. Prediction and expectation are powerful systems that contain the rules we live by. Gravity can cause you to fall from a tree. Once you have tested and acquired such a rule, you live by it forever after. Science has hard and fast rules; social networks have very different rules. The laws of physics are not negotiable; physics always wins. The rules of social engagement are negotiable and will likely change over your lifetime. Not only do your own circumstances change, but accepted social practices may change as well. For the most part, the rules you live by are acquired during childhood and adolescence, and prepare you for independent life. They are remarkably useful. If you do not have to check every assumption every time, you can choose to tune out the extraneous environment and focus your attention. You can read a book on a busy train, do work in a committee meeting, ride a mountain bike down a twisty trail.

The information on which prediction is based is refreshed constantly by the passage of time and season, changes in weather, the latest email and each new encounter. It cycles constantly from awareness to consciousness to the unconscious mode, and back again.

The predictions and expectations we rely on are also the basis for every magic trick, bit of misdirection, optical illusion and deliberate deception. Once you understand what part of prediction or expectation has been defied, an entirely new picture emerges. Years ago I watched a television series about street magic, and I was astonished at the number of ways in which the everyday matrix of expectations could be subverted. If you have ever been fooled by a lie or taken in by a deliberate con, you have bumped up against someone's manipulation of prediction and expectation. Gavin de Becker (1997) built a career and a best selling book around exactly this topic.

Sacks (2017) wrote an essay on the emergence of creative solutions. In The Creative Self (pp 129-148) he describes the manner in which the unconscious processes information. There is, he wrote, a period of subconscious incubation, an active and personal assimilation of consciously developed material that leads to reorganization and synthesis into something uniquely one's own (p.140). Sacks described the experiences of the mathematician Henri Poincaré as he struggled and failed to solve mathematical problems. On separate occasions, after a long period of conscious effort, and while occupied with some mundane task, he was struck suddenly with a brief and concise answer accompanied by immediate certainty that the answer was the correct one (p.144).

Paul Muldoon interviewed Sir Paul McCartney at length about his prolific songwriting ability. In their book, The Lyrics, (2021) Muldoon quotes McCartney as saying, "It's not so much that I compose songs, they arrive".

Information may abruptly enter awareness in a form that feels new, useful or interesting, as ideas. The sudden arrival of an idea is a curious phenomenom. When unconscious information becomes conscious, in new and meaningful patterns as an idea, it suggests very different processes at work than in the conscious mind. Somehow the unconscious mind is able to develop novel configurations of information that serve a conscious purpose. It is interesting that Sacks and Poincaré both refer to the products of the unconscious (retrieved memory and solution to a problem) as having a subjective sense of truth. The answers were immediate, vivid, and real. Poincare checked his work and Sacks had a conversation with his brother. In each case, using external methods of proof allowed them to differentiate certainty from reality.

Ideas are a product of unconscious processing. They are the stuff we use to build our world. They begin and end in consciousness, in a system that processes raw data first by the senses, and then by cognitive functions. This is information, and it is then packed as lightly or densely as our abilities permit and transferred as memory to a type of mental location that is inaccessible to awareness. We tend to think of the unconscious as a storage device, a library, where everything is kept in musty vaults until we need to recall the information again from memory. At that point we can call up someone's name, a place we went, people we saw, the times tables, how to operate a manual clutch in a car or whatever information we need.

In addition to what we think we need are the things we get, in the form of the spontaneous emergence of ideas. Ideas are the products from the unconscious portion of a mental information processing system. When we are considering how to do something, mulling over a problem, trying to figure out what to do about a situation, ideas arise. There are little ones bubbling up constantly, and big ones coming along, perhaps only a few in a lifetime. They are unique, individual, and come packaged with meaning and import. They show up to solve problems we did not always know we were thinking about. Memory is one aspect of this information system; ideas are the evidence of other ways the system works. Ideas are accompanied by emotions, such as satisfaction or wonder or happy resolution. Clarity. Sometimes, dread. They are solutions built by the unconscious to address conscious problems.

So, information from the unconscious emerges in the form of a new pattern of information, now accompanied by a sense of possibility or conviction. It is a valence of reality, ranging from this might be real, to this is true.

Sacks (2017) makes another point about the way in which we record events in memory, and that is such recordings are highly personal. The event is experienced and constructed subjectively. The unconscious mind is personal and subjective, and is not shared, but the contents of the conscious mind can be shared. The subjective experience includes an aspect of reality and truth. The product of the unconscious may feel true, yet it does not always match with external versions of the same thing. It is a fresh assemblage of information and it now has a feeling attached. The conscious mind has to determine whether it will accept, without question, the version of reality presented by the unconscious, or investigate it further, by comparing the internal sense of belief with external facts.

Sacks and Poincaré both refer to their experiences as having a subjective sense of truth. Poincaré and Sacks both were willing to take the next step and check the product. Poincaré did the work to prove his idea; Sacks had a conversation with his brother. In each case, using additional and external methods of proof allowed them to differentiate personal truth from reality. It is quite remarkable that their own minds delivered something that was so convincingly real and true. In Sacks' case, what felt real did not meet the test of external facts. In Poincaré's case, he did the work to prove his mathematical case. It would seem that there are two versions of truth, the internal felt reality and the externally verified reality.

The internal conviction of truth may be tentative, as in, an idea to be tested, or absolute. The ring of truth, even if faint, is a marker for unconscious contents arriving in consciousness.

These novel configurations of information serve a purpose. Ideas can produce other ways of doing things. They may represent an unexpected insight to an unvoiced observation that something was clumsy, just not right, or not as good as it could be. The object may be a piece of machinery, an argument in a book or interactions amongst people.

Many years ago I went on a long weekend country jaunt with a group of friends. Some were with spouses, some were solo. One of the newer members of our group, the husband of one of the core group, had been a policeman for many years. During the weekend he told his wife, after observing this group, that two members of the group, both married, were having an affair. The quiet response amongst a few of us was, no, that absolutely can not be true. No. Well, yes, it was, as became obvious several months later. The policeman said it was his job to size up people and know who was allied with whom in a group. He had a fresh take on a configuration of behaviours that was being played out in front of the rest of us, and he knew he was right. He had the same information as the rest of us, but when he put it together he had a fresh insight. In effect, he acted as the unconscious for the rest of the group.

The unconscious mind actively builds mental patterns out of information. We variously call these patterns knowledge or instinct. The patterns reflect the processes by which they were originally structured: linear, spatial, similarity or association. This internal and automatic organization of observations, facts and incidental impressions forms a knowledge base, and it is this base upon which expectation and prediction operates. When the activity of pattern building achieves a result that satisfies, it may emerge as an idea, inspiration or solution to a problem, but it appears with a sense of truth.

The end result may or may not be tested by the conscious mind. Is this solution real? Does the idea have merit? Can such a structure be built? Can I translate the music I hear into the instrument? Did that really happen? Where does this fit in my overall sense of things?

The activities we can reasonably attribute to unconscious processing include not just storage, but re processing. Information of all kinds, acquired skills, experience and procedures, is stored in the manner in which the raw data was processed. This includes visual memory such as places, faces and art; auditory memory such as for voices and music; spatial memory, such as for way finding and landmarks; language memory such as for words and rules of grammar; skilled movement such as sport and dance; emotions and events; linear, factual knowledge such as the times tables, the periodic table and the taxonomy of plants.

Once stored, information undergoes additional unconscious processes of sorting, patterning and re organizing.

All of this is based on observations of the ways in which information is changed in its journey from learning to memory and back again. While it is a reasonable guess that information is encoded and stored in these ways, the actuality is, as Schacter (1999) points out, uncertain: we guess but we do not know. Some believe that everything and everybody we encounter in our lives will be filed away in memory, not just once but repeatedly, in different categories and modalities.

There is one way to assess ideas, insights and memory, and that is to take it into the real world and check. Ask family members if there was a bomb in the garden; build the structure and see if it works; publish the paper; wait for the illicit couple to declare themselves.

Some information transfer from unconscious to conscious is automatic, accurate and fast; some is effortful, incomplete, perhaps faulty and some seems to undergo some additional reconfiguration before surfacing. One way in which information becomes active in the conscious mind is in the form of prediction.

Prediction refers to the use of stored knowledge to support everyday tasks. Prediction theory argues that a function of the unconscious is to create a pattern, map or topography, of what the sensory apparatus should be perceiving. One example is the blind spot in the visual field, of which we have no conscious awareness. Another example is the illusion of a missing limb in phantom limb pain. Optical illusions are based on the expectation of what should be there, as opposed to the visual presentation which is there.

Prediction is so powerful that it creates a type of conceptual mirage. The mirage obscures the boundary between unconscious activity and awareness. It is accepted without question; the prediction is believed.

Could the process of bringing unconscious information into consciousness involve a binding agent to reassemble disparate elements, an integrative 'glue' with the signal of accuracy? This is reminiscent of the split brain patients in which the left brain, with all confidence, pieces together different fragments into a story which is reported with conviction as true. One might also wonder if such a mechanism might be a necessary part of prediction. In prediction, the unconscious assembles information held in storage about the environment and presents it as a true representation of the surroundings to the conscious mind. The job of the unconscious is not just to build a story, but to sell it convincingly to the conscious mind.

If the peripheral world is a prediction, a complex illusion if you will, why the conviction of reality? The compelling acceptance of a percept or thought as real is a signature not only of prediction, but of unconscious activity.

Prediction, if unquestioned, is valuable. When we are young we are still learning what to expect in the world. Learning about gravity and muscle control means falling down stairs and out of trees. As we age, our ability to form complex predictions of the world increases. We get better at being on autopilot to navigate stairs and trees because we have accumulated more experience. We may then acquire experience in navigating office politics. It is this accumulation of unconscious stored experience, skills and knowledge which provides the basis for the acquisition of ever more detailed content. The unconscious holds patterns of knowledge and experience that help the aware mind recognize and understand its perceptions. The familiar becomes background, allowing the limited resources of the aware mind to attend to the novel.

For example, information on spatial relationships and topography such as the elevation of hills, familiar landmarks, and the location of one's elbows is also acquired and stored for future use. As an adult, you do not need to first locate your elbow before pulling on a shirt. The topographical and spatial maps made available by the unconscious are superimposed on the conscious sensorium, awareness, and become the reality. It is possible to walk through the house reading email on your phone; The inner map takes over and predicts where to place your foot next. The prediction model is based on what it knows, and it does not know that the cat is asleep on the floor. Our attention is not focussed on the environment, but we do not feel the lack of attention. The unconscious prediction, a type of virtual reality map, is active and we act accordingly. So does the cat, by the way.

The cycle goes on continuously. You may, upon awakening, be momentarily disoriented, but that will quickly clear as the prediction function asserts place and time. We do live in such a constant state of knowledge of our place and context that we take it for granted. Prediction is highly reliable.

Information does not persist beyond the mind unless we do something with it. We take it as given that much, if not all, of our experience in life is in storage of some sort. The unconscious not only stores, but manages information and knowledge. It feeds that content forward to the conscious mind, by way of prediction and expectation; as needed, according to the context, for a response; upon request and when triggered by specific stimuli. The conscious mind uses that content as rules to live by, to guide behaviour, to improve new learning, to efficiently perform the tasks of everyday life, and sometimes to answer questions and solve problems.

CHAPTER 6: THE BEST FIT TEST

I WANT to return to Sacks' (2017) description of Poincaré's solutions. In these experiences, Poincaré has pondered a mathematics puzzle for months. Abruptly an answer arrives in his awareness that is complete and accompanied by a conviction that it is true.

The subjective sense of breakthrough, an answer that fits the problem, is not rare. It accompanies solutions to problems of all types and sizes. "Oh, I know..." is heard all the time. I know the answer to the word problem. I know how to fix that thing. I know who dunnit. These are ideas, and they emerge fully formed into awareness.

Ideas are the evidence of the types of change that information undergoes when out of consciousness. In the previous chapter I considered different types of reorganizational processes. This re sorting might be better described as a best fit process, wherein new information is processed with test algorithms such as true/not true and useful/ not useful, in order to determine if information is to be kept or discarded, or stored and in which categories. You can think of it as a kind of perpetual Tetris game.

In that case, information is sorted outside of awareness based on the core principles the unconscious uses to make sense of the world. There is more than one core principle. Some are emotion based and some are cognitive based. Psychiatry and clinical psychology have worked with this principle extensively. The behaviours of an infant can be traced back to needs for security and bonding. The behaviours of an adult can be traced back to their experiences with security and bonding, or formative experiences of neglect. Later on, core emotional experiences of life threatening events or prolonged experiences of support and kindness can also shape core principles.

The unconscious also has cognitive core principles, and these are based on what is learned from life's experiences. These principles reflect not just experience but also the type and degree of education and access to information. These basics will determine how a chemist approaches and ultimately understands a new phenomenom, and that in turn will differ from the understanding a psychologist will bring to the same information. Based on adult behaviour, it is safe to assume that both cognitive and emotional core principles are at work in the same person. I assume that core cognitive principles operate the same way as emotional principles.

The core principles operate like a seed crystal, upon which other pieces of raw data and information can coalesce. The process of integrating new information into an existing knowledge base is similar in that for the new information to persist, it needs to fit into a structure. A narrative perhaps, similar items or similar concepts. This occurs at an unconscious level and may be quick or slow. In some complex systems it may be necessary to learn an array of facts by rote before the whole thing settles into a pattern. I am reminded of a giant chart of the Krebs Cycle I saw years ago. The Krebs Cycle is a complex cycle of chemical reactions that are the major source of energy in living organisms. The pattern and internal logic is apparent once all of the individual steps are considered together.

There may be more than one organizing principle that is attractive to the new information; it may need to be stored multiple times. The paradigm that accumulates the most information will have the greater sway in generating predictions in the real world consciousness. It is not unlike the old saying, be careful which wolf you feed. The idea is that you have competing wolves in your world. One is evil and will devour you; the other one is good and will help you. The one you feed the most with your thoughts and feelings is the one that grows stronger.

Multiple principles may be the reason why people can be ambivalent about something. There may be competing principles upon which to base understanding. This is why scientists can be persons of faith. It is not a contradiction; it reflects the reality of multiple cognitive and emotional core principles.

The process of seeking cognitive connections in pieces of information is also evident in a conscious process. When I am doing this silently, I refer to it as "noodling around in my head". I watch others carry out the same exercise while speaking. "Thinking out loud" is a verbal technique for trying out links between pieces of information. As soon as one link is made, connections to other pieces of information can be attempted.

This conscious, cognitive version of seeking a best fit is rather like brain storming. A group begins with a core concept or problem and starts trialling fits with other pieces. How does this work? Does this fit? Would this work?

These are all processes of working out a best fit for information, skills, experiences: everything we store unconsciously. The best fit becomes the most robust and enduring fit.

I want to again return to Poincaré's experience of the answer to the mathematical problem. The other very interesting part was how it felt: the answer carried a conviction of truth and accuracy. It was the answer. It was right.

Ideas can emerge into awareness with a sense of meaning or truth or both. "Meaning" is a quality of best fit. "Truth" is also a quality of best fit, but with subtle differences. The former is more emotion based; the latter is more fact based. Both are ways of organizing experience, and both reflect a degree of best fit around core principles. In Poincaré's case, the core principle was cognitive in nature, and the accompanying subjective sense was of truthfulness. Perhaps it is a case of, the better the cognitive fit at the unconscious level, the greater the conviction of truthfulness.

Consider also the experience of meaningfulness. For an experience or piece of information to have meaning, it must connect with a core principle. Meaning describes the matrix of associations with a piece of information.

When cognitive information emerges into awareness, it is accompanied by a sense of more or less truthfulness. Recall of events, or episodic memory, involves recreating or reassembling a memory. As Sacks pointed out, the reassembled memory of an event has a strong sense of truth. Poincaré's sudden realization of the solution to his problem was also accompanied by a sense of truth. Many illusions, such as the desert mirage, are accompanied by a conviction of reality. False information can be implanted to create false memories, but such memories are ultimately experienced as real. What is this conviction, this sense that the experience is accurate, real and true?

When information leaves awareness and recedes to the unconscious, we call it learning. Feelings, habits, events, education are all entries into the unconscious library. When that same information returns to consciousness, we call it memory. Depending on the form that memory takes, it may be more or less accurate, automatic and trusted. We tend to believe our memories.

The sense of certainty that accompanies memory can be nuanced, from unquestioned belief to skepticism. For the most part, we rely on memory to guide our conscious thoughts and acts. We need to rely on memory in order to function. We need to rely on the automatic, unconscious flow of information and expectation that is prediction. There simply is not enough time and mental energy to question all the information that we use: the laws of physics, our location and time frame, our physical reality. Some emotional expectations, such as the way others will treat us, are another case. If our place in a social order is threatened, if a partner or family member abruptly ceases to behave as expected, or to pass away unexpectedly, the resulting disruption in our mental state can be devastating. One's world can feel as though it is falling apart based only on changes in bonds and social connection. Imagine the effect of questioning reality itself; it would be a crippling burden, affecting the capacity to function.

Learning and recall are two phases of processing the same information. The transition from one phase to the next may not yield consistently accurate results. Sometimes you remember, sometimes you forget. Some information is recalled quickly and with certainty; other emerges with effort. What is recalled from memory falls on a gradient from reliable to error prone. The most reliable and durable outputs are prediction, the expectations we rely on to operate in the world; procedure, the routinized tasks that are energy and time savers; and habit, the quickest and least processing intensive response to a situation. Moving further down the gradient from most reliable to more error prone, are facts and pieces of information, the data points we need at any given point in time and place, and events we have experienced. Each step along the gradient is less automatic and more prone to error than the last. But at each level of accuracy, there is some element of certainty. The more automatic and accurate the information flow, the stronger the certainty in its truth. This quality of conviction is a signature of unconscious activity. It accompanies information that moves from unconscious storage to consciousness. Even erroneous contents such as delusions are held firmly, with conviction.

The literature on implanted false memories illustrates the point. Loftus and Pickrell (1995) conducted the seminal studies on implanting false memories. In the famous "lost in the mall" studies, participants were told they were in a study that looked at the ability to recall four childhood events. Three of the four events were supplied by a family member; the fourth was a false story of being lost in a shopping mall or store. The participants were provided with booklets describing briefly the four events, reportedly from their childhood as relayed by their family member, and instructed to write down their own memory of each of the four events. After they completed the task and mailed the booklet back to the researchers, they were invited in for an interview. At the interview, they were instructed to recall as much detail of the events as they could. The participants were asked to return in a few weeks for a second similar interview. In that study, 6 of the 24 participants recalled the mall story and provided additional details to flesh out the account given to them by the researchers. To one degree or another, they all reported some certainty about their memory.

The singular thing about this study was the ease with which a false memory could be implanted, using suggestion alone. The participants were told that their family member had supplied the details of the event. They were given several opportunities to remember the event. Two elements were present: the account was provided by a family member, and the participants were prompted on several occasions, over a period of time, for their recall. It is actually a very simple process. The ingredients are just repetition, narrative, and a reason to accept the narrative.

There is a phenomenom in psychological research called the feeling of knowing. This is the ability to express knowledge about unrecalled information (Schacter, 1983). It is a subjective experience, as is the feeling of awareness. One might even say it is implicit knowledge not yet overtly expressed. Koriat (2000) concluded that the feeling of knowing reflects a separate process.

It is not an attribute of the memory itself, nor is it related to the ease by which the memory can be accessed.

I think the feeling of knowing is related to the sense of certainty that accompanies a memory. Both seem to be an overlay of meaning associated with a specific piece of information.

If you have laboured over a problem, you may have a eureka type moment in which the answer comes to you in a flash. Such an answer is often material you already knew, but configured differently. The new pattern provides an answer to the problem. In common parlance one can speak of leaving problems on the back burner, or think of it another day. There are many ways in which people deliberately stop thinking of a problem, leave it to some other mechanism to solve, or even specifically pose a question, confident that an answer will arise from some source. It is tempting to suggest that these are all mechanisms by which a question or problem is left to unconscious processing. The response, if one comes, involves material already in memory that has undergone reorganization. It emerges into awareness accompanied by a sense of truthfulness or accuracy. The answer feels right, or a good fit.

As the process did not occur in awareness, we can presume this is an element of unconscious information processing. It also seems that, since the insight or answer is in relation to conscious effort, that the unconscious has responded to a conscious question with an answer. The question may be as innocuous as, what happened that day? or more profound, such as, what are the cognitive operations of the unconscious mind? Either way, there are suggestions that the unconscious mind will generate an answer, and it will ring true.

The "ring of truth" feels like a satisfactory fit. It is compelling. It is accepted in the conscious mind without question. It may be a memory, like Sacks', of the bomb in the garden; it may be Poincaré's mathematics answer.

This additional quality of truth, or reality, emerges after information has made the transition from conscious to unconscious and back to consciousness. I think of it as a process of adding meaning, and I think it is an automatic and unconscious operation.

What is this overlay of meaning? In some cases you see that an idea or inspiration is compellingly true; it has the ring of truth. In other cases it feels more like an interesting idea to be tried. It may also feel like a nonverbal sense of warning or unease, if there is a big enough disconnect between what is presented as true compared to what is already known.

The unconscious mind processes information, using sorting mechanisms. The process of sorting might include a set of algorithms that test information. One test might be true/not true. Others might be useful/not useful and pertinent/not pertinent. Depending on the complexity of the task, the process can be slow or fast. The algorithms are looking for the best fit for a piece of information. Something you see may be so similar to something you have seen before that there is no real question of identity. Yes, that is a red cardinal in winter, I have seen lots, done. On the other hand, I saw a very strange bird on my deck one winter's day and that took a fair amount of time to determine I had never seen such a bird before. With some research I was able to identify it as a type of highly bred show bird, not a wild local species at all. It was probably an escapee. The process went on until a determination had been made: no, it was not familiar, no, it was not local, no, it was not wild.

Perhaps meaning is a subjective sense of the best fit process. Certainty accompanies a strong fit; acceptance for a next level fit; unease or uncertainty for a low level fit.

A true/not true algorithm seems highly adaptive. Everything we see, learn and think on a daily basis needs to be tested for accuracy and reliability. The process may start with a simple fit test. Does this new information fit with what is already in the library? The question of goodness of fit brings in an important criterion of truth. Is the fit good enough for a "true" designation, or is the fit poor enough to result in a "not true" designation?

The information that is designated as true can be retained as a reliable element for prediction and expectation. A not true designation may not be discarded immediately, but it may be made available to the aware mind for further analysis and investigation. The need to know principle may assist in making the designation conscious, depending on the questions raised either in the conscious mind or by the environmental circumstances.

When information has gone through such a process and been deemed true, it ceases to be information and becomes knowledge. We know that memory consolidation occurs in sleep. What is learned one day is better recalled and used after a good night's sleep. The process of a true/not true test would be an interesting candidate for the energetic mental processes that occur in sleep.

The mind has mechanisms to acquire information and we tend to think the conscious mind is in control of what we learn, how we remember it and how we apply the knowledge we have gained. The conscious mind does the things of which we are aware. As a neuropsychologist, I studied these processing systems in depth. But these things are just the start of this process. Awareness is just the tip of the iceberg.

Information circulates through the mind's information processing systems, from conscious to unconscious and back again. We look closely at the learn and recall cycle we call memory in great detail. That presupposes that this is the prize, the system we can make work for our conscious purposes. There is another system of information processing that is right under our noses: ideas. Ideas are the unconscious system for answering conscious questions. It does not matter if the question is big ("how does gravity work"? Newton asks.) or small ("how to I fit one extra task into a day already full?" asks a harried manager). It does not matter the question. Once raised in consciousness, the unconscious begins to process an answer. It may take years or seconds. This mechanism operates outside of awareness and we barely give it much thought. We rely on it and take it for granted, but it is one mechanism of unconscious processing.

The unconsciously developed answer does not tell you something you did not already know: it shows, by rearranging patterns, what you already knew.

We are most aware of the conscious system, in which we ask, how can I solve this problem? This system relies on the known conscious cognitive processes and resources to answer the question. Research or collaboration or searching or trial and error building, all of these methods are performed in full awareness, as acts of will.

The other side is not conscious and since we can not see into it, we tend to dismiss it. Some speak in terms of "asking the universe", leaving it up to a metaphysical process, expressing the idea that we, as conscious beings, are not in charge of this particular way of coming at problems. It is a way of dealing with something that is not in our conscious control, but it is still ourselves working on the question out of awareness, in the unconscious system. Because there is no awareness of the way that information re enters the conscious mind from the unconscious, it is experienced as sudden, out of the blue, "as if by magic". That is not an expression of mysticism; it is an expression of the limited range of awareness. Awareness is active only in a small scope of attention; the territory of the unconscious is larger. It seemingly is not hampered by a limited attention span, so it has more resources to work with when it sets to solve a problem. That type of process does take more time.

The mind has two phases, the conscious and the unconscious. Each processes information differently. One has the facility of awareness, which is the system that handles raw data, cognitive functions and external, world based constructions such as systems of knowledge. This system manages investigation, exploration and analysis. It works with a very limited range of attention. The other system operates outside of awareness and manages the patterns of information that the aware system has built. It yields ideas, certainty, belief. It does not produce new knowledge, it reconfigures knowledge already held. It shows us what we already knew, but of which we were not aware. It does provide us with our own personal version of reality.

These re-sorted bits and pieces are what we refer to as ideas, inspirations, solutions and convictions. This is what we believe to be true, or an idea of what might be true.

The unconscious mind spontaneously integrates new information according to the core principles upon which the conscious mind will operate. As with the formation of crystals, the unconscious mind sorts new information, looking for the best possible fit of new with old. The goal is an ever more complex structure of information which will do the best job of predicting what the conscious mind can expect.

Section 4
The Nautilus

CHAPTER 7: THE ROLE OF CONSCIOUSNESS I: EXPLORATION

THE NAUTILUS is a sea creature that spends its life time moving, consuming, and building an ever increasing shell of progressively larger chambers. It as a metaphor for the process we go through in life, acquiring experience and information to build an ever increasing body of knowledge in which we reside.

THE POINT of the metaphor is that inevitably the human mind accumulates knowledge over its lifetime. The two phases of mind form a structure that supports the ongoing expansion of information. The conscious and unconscious phases of cognition act in sequence to build a data rich knowledge base that we carry all our lives, and rely upon to navigate the world.

These next two chapters look at the implications of an information processing cycle on conscious behaviour. The mind's cognitive processes, conscious and unconscious modes both, are constantly processing raw sensory data, and then integrating and organizing the resulting information. The conscious mind is not aware of many of these functions, as its role is more acquisition, less sorting and reconfiguration. It does not even have direct access to many of these functions. The conceptual picture of an information system in which consciousness is only one, perhaps small, part simply does not fit with the subjective sense of consciousness as an active, even busy, theatre of function.

We tend to think of consciousness as the most important function of our mind. For about eight hours out of every 24, consciousness and conscious activity is turned off. Consciousness is periodically dispensable to our overall health and quality of life (Walker, 2017). It is not the be all and end all. Consciousness must periodically go off line.

In earlier chapters we saw that there is far more processing and thinking occurring outside of awareness than is obvious to conscious introspection. What becomes apparent is that in awareness, we are unable to appreciate much of anything outside the immediate range of focus and span of attention. That background of activity generates a mirage that allows us to focus optimally, free of distractions. Prediction is a mechanism by which the unconscious mind provides a believable context of expectations. The prediction function is a very reliable and complex function. I expect it is resource intensive.

Awareness is a cognitive function that is tuned to the input of the sensory apparatus. It alerts to novelty in the environment and focusses attention there. The cognitive operations of consciousness are directed at processing information in the external world, but not a great deal more. Consciousness does not have a window into the day to day operations of running the body. It never sees where information goes or how it is managed once it has been acquired. It may ask for some information, but it is not in charge of the systems that bring information back from storage into awareness. Its job is elsewhere. In order to do that job most efficiently, it is told what to expect, and given the equipment and directives to acquire and build more knowledge. It is not unlike the organization around heads of state or complex organizations, in which support staff take over many routine functions leaving the head of state or CEO free to do their job. What is it about conscious cognitive functions that merits so much protection and support?

Let us begin with a very wide angle view of what people consistently do.

Humans are curious. They investigate and explore. The human nervous system responds to novelty and people react to the unexpected. The unexpected includes failures of prediction, when anything in the environment contradicts what is predicted. People are attracted to the unknown and love a mystery. Their innate and powerful sense of curiosity takes multiple forms. It can be in the form of physical exploration of new places. Curiosity drives analysis and science. It underpins the trial and error approach and the desire to see what is over the next hill.

Satisfying curiosity requires information and methods. These goals are met by bringing in the conscious cognitive functions of attention, memory, intellect, organizing, planning, spatial sense, motor and sensory perceptions.

Baars (see, for example, 2005, 2017) proposed the theory that awareness occurs where attention is focussed. "Global Workspace Theory (GWT) can be compared to a theater of mind, in which conscious contents resemble a bright spot on the stage of immediate memory, selected by a spotlight of attention under executive guidance. Only the bright spot is conscious; the rest of the theater is dark and unconscious" (Baars, 2017).

The cognitive functions of the conscious mind are ways to search out raw data and process it into useful information. The primary function is attention, and awareness occurs where attention is placed. It is a limited and tightly focussed activity, fenced in by prediction and directed by goals. There are limits to the time frame and span of attention. It is incapable of attending to all the content stored in the unconscious, and the entire range of sensory data in the external world, and still carry out activities in that limited focus. Search and process takes up much of its bandwidth.

What will activate awareness in the first place? Curiosity about unknowns in the external world will trigger a response. Awareness is reliably generated by failures of prediction.

The conscious mode is active not just in the immediate dimension of awareness, but in a wider stage of potential, waiting to be triggered. The cognitive functions are available at a moment's notice to process some novelty. In addition there is a whole set of cognitive operations devoted to planning. These activities start with goals and contain multiple pathways of thinking and activity. Neuropsychology has tests to investigate this set of functions. It includes sorting: what goes where?, and sequencing, what goes first and second and so on? They include timing, contingencies and initiation. These functions are in general described as executive functions and a large portion of brain anatomy supports them. Many of these functions can be interrupted or lost in cases of injury to the frontal lobes, the anterior portion of the brain. They handle motor programs, in which a set of movements are lined up in sequence awaiting the correct circumstances to be set off. Training in science and logic sets up a series of cognitive steps by which problems can be addressed. Such a cognitive sequence, once developed, is an available set of programs that can be run as needed.

Amongst this set of programs are goals. The goals reflect individual circumstances, experience and knowledge. It can be the basic need to find some way to survive, or a desire to solve a mathematics problem. When the frontal lobes are affected by injury or disease, the consequent deficits can include problems developing goals, or maintaining motor activity. Patients with parkinsonian syndromes may have trouble rising out of a chair or walking more than a few steps. Patients with frontal lobe involvement may have trouble initiating activities; they appear apathetic, or they may lose spontaneity. They may lose the ability to analyze a task or plan an activity, or even to anticipate the impact of their actions.

Many cognitive functions and much brain territory is devoted to setting and achieving goals. These are available in the larger realm of consciousness, awaiting the proper trigger to be activated in full awareness.

The drives and goals of any given person arise from a variety of external and internal needs. Conscious cognitive functions are brought to bear on the goals and drives that are dominant. I propose that conscious cognitive functions reduce to two broad categories of activities in the service of goals: learn and create. In order to learn new things, one must explore the unknown. This chapter focusses on the very broad category of learning.

There is always a reason to acquire more information, whether it is a drive to satisfy curiosity or an immediate goal of building a better shelter. Awareness happens when attention is drawn to something. At that point, novelty is evaluated. If no further attention is necessary, attention focusses elsewhere. If further attention is warranted then curiosity, investigation, exploration and analysis are all potential responses. Those activities will result in something learned.

What if the environment is so predictable that there is nothing new to be learned? Several responses are possible, but restlessness is one of them. If this cycle is playing out in a child, random curiosity leads to exploration and experimentation. What is on the shelf in the closet? What happens if I take the telephone apart? What type of response can I get by pinching the baby? In young adults the restlessness and curiosity takes the forms of investigation and travel. What is over that range of mountains? What books are in the library? In older people it may take the form of peering out the window, wondering what the neighbours are doing. It is a clear sign of something wrong when someone is so withdrawn and apathetic that novelty will not elicit a response of some kind.

The cognitive functions all address the unknowns of raw sensory input. Sensory systems will describe the ways a thing looks, sounds and feels. Language will give it words to describe its attributes and generate a name. Language will also provide a narrative that places the thing in context. Spatial systems will define location, size and movement. Motor systems will identify how to physically interact with the thing. Executive functions will plan more activities, experiments or investigations. Memory will store the experience.

Whether the urge to learn something arose from an internal drive or external source, the process is the same. There is curiosity, investigation and analysis. Cognitive processing produces information. Whatever is learned eventually recedes from awareness, presumably bound for storage in the unconscious.

From a neuropsychology perspective, the brain is constantly processing information, from the easily accessible conscious mode, through the black box of the unconscious mode, and back again. Conscious processing occurs in a variety of cognitive domains, but the end product is something that is more complex than the information at the starting point. The process repeats, constantly.

The constant repetition is also interesting. Certainly, life is full of mysteries and challenges that elicit the focussed attention of awareness. One cannot easily assume that the external world is the only source of inspiration. This information model can also make sense if one assumes that the unconscious drives the conscious mind to seek out and develop new knowledge. The evolutionary strategy might be summed up as this: knowledge is power.

Consciousness is not just a step in an information processing system, but the place where the search for information occurs. The unconscious may process whatever information comes its way, but it is the conscious mind that is equipped to go looking for more. Consciousness is the place where the drive of curiosity is able to get to work with investigation, exploration, analysis and construction. The conscious mind has a set of tools that function precisely to process raw data into meaningful information. This is what it does.

The most important tool that the aware mind has at its disposal is the cognitive function of attention. When attention is focussed anywhere, an idea, a perception of something in the environment, an event requiring response, or other cognitive functions can be activated into awareness and brought to bear. Conscious cognition begins with attention.

The clinical neuropsychological examination occurs precisely under these conditions. The subject's attention is focussed on a specific set of commands given by the examiner. Anything that might distract from attention is minimized. The room is quiet, phones are turned off, the examiner verifies that the subject is awake, alert, not under the influence of intoxicants and is able to attend normally. Everything begins with attention.

At that point the neuropsychologist can evaluate the cognitive functions that we are able to use consciously. In broad but not exhaustive terms, the domains are learning and memory, language, spatial perception, intelligence, motor skills, sensory perception, and the so called executive skills such as organization, planning, switching and focussing attention, categorizing and sequencing. The neuropsychological exam investigates cognition that occurs in full awareness. Cognitive functions that are presumed to operate outside of awareness, such as incidental learning, may be identified but are not the point of the examination. The focus is on the functions that can operate in full awareness. These are the tools of the conscious mind.

To what end are these conscious tools employed? Consider what happens in awareness: curiosity, exploration, investigation, analysis, building and creating. Each cognitive domain contributes processing capability to the same goal: turn raw environmental data into patterns of information.

Again, look at the tools available: memory, language, spatial perception, executive functions, sensation, motor skills and intelligence. The universal activities that employ these tools are exploration, learning and creating.

I first thought about these issues as I learned about the development of hominids, likely many species of them, that spread from Africa throughout the rest of the world. I was struck with the question of why people kept moving around. It looked like a near universal activity. A search for scarce resources is certainly a reasonable hypothesis, but I suspect it can not entirely explain that much movement. I think exploration is the norm, not the exception. I also think an important driver to all this movement is curiosity. Children, adults, all exhibit a drive to know more, see further, experience more, understand better. This one thing underlies vast amounts of human activity. What is the link?

Curiosity drives learning. Cognitive functions are the tools that take the information found by curiosity and process it into patterns that we call knowledge.

Transforming data into patterns can be simple or complex. Motor responses to sensory stimuli can be very simple linkages, but the result is something learned. Similarities link observations. Language sets pieces of information together in narratives, and narratives are powerful learning devices. Things that occur together are learned as a set. The same stars, seen each night, together in the same place, are learned as a configuration. Patterns feel meaningful, and meaning is another powerful tool for learning and memory. Linking things by meaning, in a sequence or narrative or visual pattern, or all three, means that far more information can now be organized, learned and retained.

As discussed in previous chapters, once something, especially a complex set of information, is learned, it passes out of awareness. The transition is automatic. The conscious mind has performed its task, and the end product leaves awareness, to be taken up by the unconscious. The conscious mind moves on to the next task, which is to find the raw data of the world and create something useful, be it a story or a structure. The focus of the conscious mind's activities is to process that raw data into information.

Neuroscience research is demonstrating that consciousness is associated with information processing. Research into levels of consciousness has led to various means by which the presence of any level of consciousness can be approximated with measures such as imaging (Owen 2017) and pulses. Stamatakis (2021) provides a nice summary of the latter line of research demonstrating that the complexity of information processing occurring in the brain relates rather well with levels of consciousness (https://theconversation.com/clues-to-consciousness-how-dopamine-fits-into-the-mystery-of-what-makes-us-conscious-podcast-169418).

Consciousness is but one facet of information processing.

Theories of consciousness such as global workspace theory address where awareness arises, that is, in the focus of attention, and how cognitive functions are brought to bear in conscious activity.

The things that are processed and learned in conscious cognition change when out of consciousness, while stored in the unconscious. What we perceive and learn is not the same information we use to predict the world, the information we use to make choices and to build or create.

If we look at the difference between information that is learned and stored, then later recalled or used, we can identify how information changes when it is out of consciousness. Very specific changes occur. Information is sorted into patterns, placed into the individual context and history, meaning is conferred, reality is reorganized and degrees of conviction are the result.

The conscious mind is not the only place where cognition occurs.

Cognition is a biphasic process; both conscious and unconscious functions are at work. Cognition operates not only with the raw sensory data of the world but also with the products of unconscious processing, such as memories, ideas and inspirations. Information circulates. The two phases of mind, conscious and unconscious, can be thought of as a cyclical process with specific activities occurring in each phase, with raw sensory data being transformed into information and then into meaningful knowledge about the world.

The two phases approach to cognition allows us to consider the interesting territory of how two people can have different, but vivid and meaningful, memories of the same event. It makes sense if you view the mind as more than an information accumulation device.

CHAPTER 8: THE ROLE OF CONSCIOUSNESS II: CREATION

AFTER EXPLORATION, the second major category of conscious activity is creation. After the conscious mind processes raw data into recognizable information, it transfers the information to the unconscious mind. There, processes take over that sort the information into categories, place it into context and apply attributes such as meaning and reliability. This integrates some of the information into knowledge.

Knowledge held only in the mind does not persist beyond the individual. If it is to be maintained, it is necessary to express it in concrete, real world terms by sharing the information beyond the individual. This takes on forms subsumed into the concept of culture, which are the ways in which a group transmits their knowledge. It includes oral and written stories, built structures and crafted tools. Oral histories can preserve knowledge long after structures fall and tools lie buried in the soil (Steeves, 2021). The creation stage of information processing is carried out consciously and with intent. The knowledge of how to knap a piece of flint into a useful hand axe is built up over hours of practice. It is a process of developing a motor skill plus trial and error for the procedure. In the end, the individual skill of building this tool becomes unconscious, but the real world result of the process of using that knowledge is a concrete representation of knowledge.

The individual process of turning information and knowledge into real world creations is the second major human activity after exploration. The process is always the same, whether the resulting knowledge is how viruses replicate, how to structure a symphony or how to govern a nation. First, curiosity, then exploration, then experimentation and creation. It is not by mistake that the core requirement for a PhD is to create a body of work that adds to the knowledge in a field. The point is to produce something new within a discipline of knowledge. A new creation, because it is new, will always pull the attention of others. People will explore new ideas and technologies the way they explore new countries and new continents. It sparks the acquisition of information in others, and the cycle of information, curiosity, exploration and creation turns again.

There is another aspect to the phase of creation. The individual absorbs learning in various forms, but the persistence of that learning depends on what can be shared and taught. Memories can be shared, but ultimately they die with the owner.

The culture of a people values knowledge, and preserving it is important for survival of the group. It is too valuable to leave to memory alone. The acts of building, writing and creating are all means to store memory beyond a human lifespan. In such a formulation, art becomes an embodiment of perception, ideas and knowledge; tools show both the method of construction but also their use. Structures demonstrate real experience in building, housing and the use of social spaces.

Built items and structures of all kinds transform the contents of mind into examples that can be shared and taught. They are a form of external memory storage. Art becomes a back up system for experience, if you will. Archaeology provides us with examples of how people reified knowledge into concrete expressions. A henge shows the place where people met to build it. Cave paintings show the animals the people knew and hunted. A hand axe, a skill built over over many iterations, exemplifies knowledge gained by practice. A Roman road is a durable example of how to build a road that holds up under heavy use.

Acquiring information is an activity of the conscious mind. The search, storage and constructive use of information, then knowledge, are all parts of the cycle and are fundamental elements of the organization of mind.

The role of the conscious mind in exploring, analyzing, constructing physical things and building information constructs are all ways to gather new information and create knowledge. The previously acquired skills and knowledge are stored unconsciously and available to the conscious mind. Every skilled practitioner, be they carpenter or molecular biologist, has learned how to use specific tools to achieve outcomes. In all cases, new knowledge is the stuff that drives the machinery of mind.

We can evaluate how the unconscious mind processes and stores information by the resulting product. It can be skill with tools, or in sports, or musical instruments or procedural memory for how to carry out a task, like setting up tests in a neuropsychology practice. The unconscious product can also take the form of episodic memory. The cases of eyewitness testimony or implanted false memories reveal what an error prone system it is. In neuropsychology, testing for incidental learning demonstrates how much information is acquired unintentionally, when learning something is beside the point.

The unconscious mind is able to absorb a wide range of material and use it to create patterns and narratives. Not all are accurate; some are even wildly inaccurate. To the holder of the memory, false memories are indistinguishable from true memories. They all serve a purpose, which is to build a matrix of information from whatever raw material is available. An internal narrative or model of the world may never be challenged, but real world creations meet real world challenges. They can be seen, used or read by others, collapse or fail in any number of ways. Logical flaws, erroneous beliefs, engineering failures all become evident.

Oliver Sacks discusses this problem in his essay, The Fallibility of Memory (Sacks, 2017, pp 101-122). False memories are not uncommon events, and feel "...vivid, detailed and concrete" (p.104). He described remembering a thermite bomb falling near his house during the World War II Blitz in 1940-41. His family corrected his recall, telling him he was not even present when the bomb fell. He felt astounded. The memory was real to him. He had apparently taken his brother's account of the event and mentally constructed his own memory. The constructed memory was indistinguishable from memories that others could validate. This is the nature of episodic memory stored in the unconscious mind, and it is not unlike the story concocted by the left hemisphere Interpreter described by Gazzaniga (1988). Accuracy is not the point or goal of this unconscious process; building a narrative is the point. This tells us something very important about unconscious processing of information. Pattern and meaning are higher priorities than accuracy. Accuracy is an attribute that arises from real world manifestation.

One might wonder if the unconscious, once unburdened with a need for literal accuracy, is thereby freed to develop novel configurations. It is interesting that Sacks (2017) and Poincaré both refer to the products of the unconscious (retrieved memory and solution to a problem) as having a subjective sense of truth: it is immediate, vivid, and real. It is also interesting to note that they checked the mental product. Poincaré did the work to prove his idea; Sacks had a conversation with his brother. In each case, using additional and external methods of proof allowed them to differentiate fantasy or fiction from reality. What is real to us is not accepted as real by the rest of the world until other people agree with it.

Truth is felt in the mind and tested in the real world.

It is the conscious mind that has the greater opportunity for accuracy, both at the intake when information can be considered at length, but also in the output, where information can be tested. The unconscious blandly consumes information, as long as it is in the form of a meaningful pattern. Aspiring athletes are aware that their learned golf swing, or cycling rhythm, is not their best, but it is what they first learned. Correcting it takes effort, and is most efficient with an outside observer. As in the case with the memory of a bomb in young Oliver's yard, in some cases it takes an outside party to find errors and provide the necessary feedback to correct them.

Knowledge is acquired by the individual but refined in the group. Take the example of science, in which the stated primary rationale is the pursuit of knowledge. A major step in reducing error is peer review. When done properly, it leads to sharing knowledge by way of publication. As politics has demonstrated, if a social or cultural group does not accept an idea or a piece of information, it can be suppressed indefinitely.

Sacks (2017) makes one more point about the way in which we record events in memory, and that is such recordings are highly subjective. The event is experienced and constructed subjectively, by individuals. Consciousness is of course subjective, individual and unique to each person.

The products of conscious information processing can be shared. We have some knowledge of the state of information in a culture before the development of written language by the remnants of things that were constructed and built. Take as an example standing stones and henges. One possible element of shared knowledge is that the henge served to mark a place where people congregated for a purpose. Early humans moved around and perhaps a henge marked a place to which the same people returned time after time. Some stones may have served only as a place marker, but in some cases complex monuments were assembled. At the simplest level, a large henge or structure means many people congregated, spent time there and organized themselves sufficiently to build a sizable structure. Orienting the entrance to the mid year solstice communicates another piece of knowledge, perhaps the time of year when they came together. There are many examples of such ancient constructions of stones found worldwide, such as in Australia (Wurdi Youang, https://arxiv. org/abs/0906.0155), England (Stonehenge), and Turkey (Gobekli Tepe).

Monuments document people, where they congregated, the tools and materials they used and perhaps how far they travelled. Some structures are thought not to be dwellings, as there are no signs of hearth, fire or food. They do communicate, to the community and anyone else, that people were there, how they built the structure and what materials they used to create the structure. Everything is information, and some of the information contained in these monuments has persisted for thousands of years.

Story telling, epic poems, legends and oral history are more examples of how a community or people retain the knowledge of their history and culture (Steeves, 2021). The verbal representation of events in memory is maintained by repetition of memorized material, and representations in drawings or art. When writing is developed it becomes possible to document more complex information, but it never replaces the purposes served by art, monuments and tools. When learning a new skill there is really no substitute for examples of how it is done.

Consciousness is one aspect of a mind that gathers information. It is curious. It explores, creates and builds. It results in an accumulation of information. This occurs with any course of study, instruction, observation or exploration.

The conscious act of creation entails acquiring skills, experience or information, so that a body of work built up consciously also resides in unconscious storage. This unconscious accumulation of information is sorted and processed. It coheres, becomes meaningful and develops its own momentum over time. There is a critical mass at which it will be expressed. This is the point where a solution to a problem, or an idea about a topic you have been pondering, will occur. This is when you realize that there is a better way to do something, or it all makes sense if you look at it from a different perspective. It is the point where you no longer try to remember piano scales or bicycle riding; the needed skill flows.

The unconscious process of sorting of course results in organization and assemblage. The process is constant and ongoing, awake and asleep. The results that have the best internal organization, or coherence, will emerge as ideas or inspiration. They are the products of unconscious cognitive processes. Extended conscious activity spurs unconscious cognitive activity.

Authors speak of characters in their novels taking on a life of their own; Sir Paul McCartney speaks of songs emerging already formed; Poincaré wrote of solutions presenting themselves, whole and complete.

There needs to be conscious work to spur on the process. The cognitive cycle is fed by conscious input of new information, already processed and presorted in modalities such as language, visuo-spatial array, sensation. Conscious information already carries attributes of time and place, colour, shape, movement, name if not verbal descriptors, before it recedes into the unconscious and undergoes yet more processing, sorting and organizing.

Section 5
Consciousness

CHAPTER 9: BUILDING KNOWLEDGE

THE NEXT two chapters consider some implications of an information cycle for consciousness, awareness and self awareness.

Consciousness acts to acquire information in the forms of experience, emotion, skill and knowledge. That information then recedes into the unconscious mind and is stored (Kihlstrom, 1987). The unconscious uses it to build and update a prediction of the real world (Wilson, 2002). The prediction provides context and guides activity or behaviour. It is a type of autopilot for everyday activity, responses and social behaviour. (Wilson, 2002).

We tend to speak of the unconscious and the conscious as two separate minds. We do not have two systems of thinking, we have one. It operates in different modes, using the same neural systems (Bargh, 2017). The conscious mind has limited attentional capacity, and a wide range of cognitive activity, but the unconscious mind appears to be able to manage even more information than the conscious mind.

This unitary mind has an information processing system in which real world data is processed by conscious cognitive operations into information, which then automatically recedes into unconscious storage. The unconscious mind takes this same information, processes it and integrates it with patterns of previously learned material. That updated knowledge base is used to inform the prediction function. This is an automatic, reliable and information intensive system. This system tells you who you are, where you are, and what you can reliably expect to happen next.

The prediction function is operational while we are awake and conscious. It is constantly receiving new information and informing us of the updated status. The information processing system is a cycle. On the conscious side, the circulation of the loop is fed by new information. That part of the loop is driven by the human attribute of curiosity. The unconscious side automatically refreshes and updates predictions.

Consciousness is a mental state hypothesized to account for wakeful interaction with the environment. It processes raw sensory data into useful information. It focusses attention on the junction of expectation and reality. Awareness is a state that arises when attention is focussed. This is the condition of being aware of something. If the prediction and the reality are congruent, there is no need to attend further. If reality and prediction are not congruent, attention remains focussed, awareness is sustained and other cognitive processes are activated. Awareness is a finite resource with a limited capacity for range and time. The predicted world is excluded from attention, and we are never aware of the boundary between reality and prediction.

Awareness is a subjective experience of information. We are aware of something. We can judge when someone is aware of something because they can explicitly state what they know. Awareness is described by Schacter and colleagues (1988) in terms of explicit knowledge. We know that we know something. We can verbalize the information and act with intention on it. Awareness responds to novelty, or new information, that which is not predicted nor expected.

The conscious mind focusses attention on information. This function of attention is limited; we call it the attention span. Nonetheless, a great deal of information can be brought into focus, chiefly by lining up information into groups and assigning one piece of information from the group the role of place holder. One method is to chunk information together into meaningful units. Each unit takes up one portion of attentional space. Advanced chess players think in terms of groups of moves, rather than a single move. Another method is to consult an external source of stored information such as a book. As one colleague said in a job interview, "I don't know the answer to your question, but I know where to look it up".

Another is to prioritize information necessary for the task at hand, recognizing that other pieces of information are present but subsidiary to the matter.

An experienced person will be able to sort useful from incidental information rapidly. As a neuropsychologist I, and all my colleagues, routinely reviewed copious medical records and associated materials in the course of conducting an assessment on a patient. Some of these files were massive, filling multiple banker's boxes of paper (back when records came on paper).

Information in that line of work, like many, is everything. Experience and skill go into choosing which information matters, and which does not. The same can be said of the human mind. While attention and awareness focus on a small range of information at any given time, the wider activity of consciousness is taking in everything else. We refer to it as incidental learning.

We experience consciousness as central to our existence. Humans have actually posed the question, If a tree falls in Siberia and there is no one around to hear it, does it make a sound? The question sums up one attitude toward human consciousness: everything that exists is in our consciousness, and if it is not in our consciousness it does not exist.

It is a faulty presumption. Yes, things exist beyond our conscious awareness. We are not physically equipped to see infrared light under normal conditions, but it exists. Most of our mental functions operate outside of consciousness, but we do not have direct experience of it.

Consciousness is a cognitive function that facilitates cognitive operations within directed attention. The boundary between conscious and non conscious functions is characterized by the infinity illusion. There is a powerful cognitive illusion, not unlike an optical illusion, that keeps us from understanding where consciousness ends and prediction begins. We can not tell where the boundary lies, between perception and the prediction our brain builds. The brain predicts what is in peripheral vision, whether we will decide someone is trustworthy, what the cake will taste like. The brain operates your body while you ride a bike, leaving you free to respond to the unexpected when necessary. Awareness, the cognitive activity wherein we focus our attention, is far more limited than we are actually able to appreciate. Because of that restriction, trying to grasp the nature of consciousness is a lot like trying to lay water pipe to a mirage in a desert.

In its' role as a processor of information, consciousness is driven by curiosity to not just passively receive, but to actively seek out additional information. This leads to investigation and exploration. In the service of those goals, a range of cognitive functions are activated in conscious awareness to process raw sensory data and thereby create information. These functions, which are available on demand to the conscious mind, are the same ones evaluated in a neuropsychological assessment. They include language and memory, visuospatial and executive functions, sensory and motor functions. These functions are the tools that permit consciousness to perceive and identify, employ complex motor actions, understand spatial information, use language to create narrative, to sort, categorize, focus and switch attention, plan sequences, create goals and run complex plans. It allows the conscious mind access to information in memory.

What happens to information once acquired? It recedes from awareness into a type of non aware storage we call the unconscious. The information that we consciously learn may not be the same as what is later recalled. There is an interim, unconscious phase in which additional processing and transformation occurs. This implies a circuit of knowledge transmission, from acquisition to storage.

The unconscious carries out a number of cognitive processes. These processes store learning as memory; seek the best fit for new information with old; create new patterns in response to need; place information in context and add meaning to patterns of information. The unconsciously developed answer does not tell you something you did not already know: it shows, by rearranging patterns, what you already knew.

Meaning and knowledge are arising all the time in awareness, in the form of ideas. Ideas can address small issues or large problems. Ideas are an answer to any question that may have presented itself, or that we pose ourselves. Ideas are a product of unconscious processing.

Independent of what we think we need or the information we ask for, are the things that just turn up. Ideas are the products of an unconscious information processing system. When we are asking ourselves a question or noticing a problem, trying to figure out what to do about a situation, sooner or later ideas arise. They come packaged with meaning and import. They show up as needed to address questions we pose or problems we did not know we were thinking about.

Such answers that arrive abruptly into awareness can feel meaningful. Meaning is a specific part of a context and could be the most important element in the creation of knowledge. Meaning is a type of glue that binds information together so that it can be learned and used. Meaning is the sense of where something fits in the overall scheme of things. Any schema can serve the purpose, such as the emotional world, the taxonomy of plants, useful information about committee structure or any organization of information that an individual has already acquired as their body of knowledge. Meaning turns information into something that can be used to guide future behaviour: knowledge.

Ideas represent information re assembled outside of awareness and into useful configurations. They are the stuff we use to build understanding and objects. They begin and end in consciousness.

This is information, and it is then packed as lightly or as densely as our individual abilities permit. We tend to think of the unconscious as a storage device, a library, where everything is kept in vaults until we need to recall the information again from memory. Then we call up information we need, such as someone's name, a place we went, people we saw, the times tables, how to operate a manual clutch in a car.

Information flows constantly into the conscious mind. The outflow of information from the unconscious can take the form of memory, meaning, ideas and prediction. Memory is one aspect of the outflow of information from the unconscious. All of these are indicators that the information system is at work. They are solutions built and presented by the unconscious to address conscious problems.

The process of building a prediction of reality requires a lot of information, and it has to be sorted and integrated at every step of the way. Gopnik (2020) uses the concept of the infant as a scientist in the crib, acquiring data points and building reality.

The cognitive cycle hypothesis predicts that a set of newly learned information will be recalled at, or more than, 24 hours embedded in a format or context specific to the individual. That means placing information into a personally meaningful or useful context. When I was in high school I learned physics as a series of formulas to be applied in specific situations. This changed when I attended university. The goal of instruction in my first year physics course was to learn the principles of physics on an intuitive level. What the instructors intended was that we could learn to progress past rote learning of formulae to understanding how to use the concepts.

What is recalled from memory will show change from the initial learning stage. Pristine, fully accurate and unembellished recall would be the exception, not the norm. The information becomes enmeshed in one's own understanding of meaning and utility.

Consciousness takes the knowledge base and uses it to satisfy curiosity with exploration and creation. That has obvious adaptive consequences. We construct a prediction of the world. With knowledge we improve the important tasks of building shelter, acquiring food, forming social bonds, developing clans and societies, and satisfying the desire for more exploration, knowledge and creation. Knowledge enhances survival. The two elements of the information processing system not only support awareness, but act together in an ongoing cycle that can take on progressively more challenging cognitive problems.

Consciousness is the cognitive function that captures and organizes information for storage and processing. As the stored information grows, more complex systems come into play. Motor functions become increasingly skilled. Vocabulary grows from simple to complex. Emotions become more nuanced. Thought patterns organize information more densely. The search for information starts immediately in life, is driven by curiosity and exploration, and becomes increasingly focussed by choices in education, life experiences and work. The end point of it all is learning. Consciousness is a tool that enhances the process.

We are very efficient learning machines. Our seemingly innate drives of curiosity and exploration advance the acquisition of information. The drive might be evident in a simple yearning for novelty, a new flavour of food, a bit of gossip or a new experience. It might be the lifelong pursuit of excellence in a talent or one area of ability. Curiosity and a desire to know more, do more, underlies our approach to anything unknown, hidden or unattainable. The things we want to learn define us as individuals. That we want to learn at all defines us more broadly.

There are some common features and patterns in conscious and unconscious information processing. Consciousness processes information, experiences it as awareness and learns it. Consciousness learns, creates and corrects. The resulting information is stored in the unconscious, where it remains available to influence future behaviour.

The unconscious does not just store knowledge, it evaluates it for best fit. The degree of fit with old learning provides a judgement of relative truth, reality and reliability. Only the best fit material goes into the prediction function, because this is what you need to believe is real.

Another way to think about the flow of information from the unconscious to the conscious phase is to assume that the prediction function is fed by a lifetime of accumulated information held in the unconscious. This would mean that there is a wealth of knowledge in the unconscious library that is available to inform the prediction function. This knowledge is implicitly available to consciousness when prediction meets reality.

CHAPTER 10: THE KNOWLEDGE CYCLE AND CONSCIOUSNESS

THIS BOOK attempts to model consciousness within a neuropsychological framework. This means thinking of consciousness and awareness as cognitive functions that process information. Following information through its iterations reveals a cycle of cognitive processing and change. Each phase of the cycle processes information differently. The conscious mind handles raw sensory data and, with cognitive tools, begins to shape a structure and narrative. It has no access to unconscious processes because it does not need access in order to perform its tasks. The unconscious processes include, storage, sorting, testing for attributes such as best fit and usefulness. It binds elements within context and provides meaning. This version of information is fed forward to the conscious mind as a template, a prediction of reality.

A cognitive based description for consciousness, awareness and unconscious processes is possible in a model of a cyclical information system. Tracking information as it proceeds from consciousness, to the unconscious and back again to consciousness highlights the changes in processing methods that occur as it travels the route. The two systems operate very differently. Awareness appears to occur where the two meet. Awareness shifts out as information moves from the conscious to the unconscious phases. Awareness shifts back in as information moves from unconscious to conscious processes.

The first big task of describing the cycle was the illusion hiding the boundary between conscious and unconscious modalities of mind, and that was addressed in the Infinity Pool section. This allows us to set aside the experiential confound of consciousness and address the functions it serves. Following the functions applied to information, the cognitive processes that occur out of awareness, in the unconscious modality of mind, were discussed in the Library and Ring of Truth sections. It becomes possible to follow the same piece of information as it moves from raw sensory data into processing as information, from re processing unconsciously into new configurations of knowledge, and used again in consciousness in the form of the prediction function, in ideas and in fueling curiosity. The idea of a cycle of cognitive functions as an accumulator of knowledge was explored in the Nautilus section.

A cycle of information management is all very interesting, but my original goal was to better understand consciousness. So, do these ideas provide any useful direction? This chapter looks at the implications of the proposed information processing loop. These include prediction, certainty, ideas, the pursuit of a stable state between reality and expectation, awareness and self awareness.

Is an information processing cycle a reasonable way to think about consciousness? The model developed here is deliberately reminiscent of other biological systems where the product of one process leads on to another process, and so on in a self reinforcing pattern or cycle. A longer description of this approach can be found in Solving for Pattern (Berry, 1981). Briefly, Berry argues that complex biological systems are composed of other, mutually interdependent, patterns. The products and needs of the systems are interlocking and mutually reinforcing. Another principle is that evolutionary biology retains successful ways of doing things. In cells and ecosystems, there are cycles of activity that transform one thing into another and reinforce the other elements of the system in doing so.

And so we can start to think about consciousness and its cognitive function of processing information in the same light. Beginning with the cognitive function of awareness, and the neuropsychological syndromes of loss of awareness, it is possible to follow the products of cognitive processes in and out of awareness. These products are linked and transformed in consciousness and unconsciousness in a self reinforcing and perpetual cycle in which consciousness plays a part in creating knowledge.

It is a very interesting exercise to follow systems in the brain that manage information. The same piece of information that starts at one point in the cycle can be quite different when the cycle returns to its starting point. The fact is that what we originally perceive in the world becomes something very different after our minds are through with it.

Here is a very minor example. Recently I had some foot pain. I remembered that I had bought a salve for plantar fasciitis a few years ago and found it helpful. I went looking for the salve. In my memory, it came in a white tube, about the same size as a large tube of toothpaste, with an orange cap. I looked everywhere for this tube, but could not find it. Two days later I stumbled across the salve I was looking for, while looking for something else. The tube of salve was small, about the size of a travel sized tube of toothpaste. It was silver, with a white cap and a blue banner at one end. There was a very small circle of orange on the label. No wonder I could not find the large white tube with an orange cap. It did not exist. The faulty memory of the tube had become the prediction of what I wanted to find. The original pieces of information were changed beyond recognition by their journey through my mental processes. What I was conscious of two years ago when I bought the salve was not the same thing I was conscious of two days ago when I searched for it. I was quite certain I knew what that tube looked like it, and I was quite wrong. Certain, but wrong.

A small but illustrative story. The same thing happens constantly in our minds. We call it confirmatory bias, or world view or prejudice, but the reality we expect is a reflection of our individual experience and rarely a fully accurate picture.

The matter of what we rely on as an accurate understanding of the world is a central and important conclusion. What we believe to be true may be wrong, but we won't have any way of knowing that until we come across proof that we have been wrong. We experience the products of our unconscious mind, the predictions and memories, with certainty, faith and conviction. We rely on them for accuracy. Our cognitive processes transform information. The prediction function takes that information and tells us what is in the world and what to expect, and we believe it to be true.

Another point is the border between awareness in the foreground and prediction in the background. I have previously made the point that awareness arises at the intersection of attention and prediction. Let's consider a few scenarios.

If I am sitting on the front porch reading a book, the prediction function includes a lawn and a tree to the side. Even though I am not looking at it, I believe it is still there. The sound of leaves moving does not draw my attention because it fulfills a reasonable expectation. I have no reason to look at the tree to make sure it is still there. The unconscious has provided this backdrop while I read, and I accept it with certainty. I believe the tree is there, and I count on the mirage to remain stable while I read.

Let's say I am sitting in a window seat on a train while I read. The prediction is that the seats, racks and aisle will all remain stable while I read, but there will be changes in the images in the window as the train moves. I can still read while the train is moving because the expectation is that the display in the window will change. In other circumstances the prediction becomes less stable and my level of certainty may change. Instead of scenery passing by the window, The train slows down and red lights are flashing in the window. Prediction plummets, certainty recedes and uncertainty is heightened. I stop reading and start attending closely to the window because prediction is failing and I need more information. If I determine that we slowed for a rail crossing in a small town, that might be enough information to bring prediction back to a stable state. I can resume reading.

De Becker (1997) describes the other aspect of this situation. I am sitting on a train, reading, but have a sense of something is not quite right. Everything is as predicted: the train is moving, I am reading, but I am uneasy. I look up to see a stranger sitting across from me, and he is staring at me. Reality has intruded on prediction with something unexpected, and I am alerted.

I have several options to bring this perturbation of prediction and expectation back into stability. I have read De Becker, I have dealt with a number of unexpected and at times threatening situations in my life. I can respond to the situation in any number of ways. I can glare, I can ask a question, I can ignore the stranger and go back to my reading. The point of any choice of behaviour is to reduce the unexpected and get back to a stable prediction state wherein I can focus my attention on my reading without distraction.

This illustrates a few points about the function of prediction. The prediction itself needs to remain stable within acceptable parameters, so that attention and awareness can continue focussing on the task at hand. The stable state is accompanied by a sense of certainty, or truth, or belief. There is no need to pay attention to the tree or the window, because I believe the backdrop that is predicted by the unconscious is true. I believe the tree is there. However, in some situations the prediction is not stable and it is accompanied by uncertainty or fear. During the omicron wave of the pandemic in 2022, there was a lack of certainty about personal safety throughout the population. There was not enough information to either our conscious or unconscious minds as to determine safety from a variety of threats, including illness, loss of income, death of loved ones, financial distress to name only a few. Learning to live with uncertainty over a long period of time required some effort. The prediction function struggled to find enough information to reach a stable state.

Prediction works for us because it provides a mirage that we believe to be true. It is a process accompanied by the attribute of certainty. The credence, certainty and sense of truthfulness is a product of unconscious processing. Certainty is a stable state and allows other functions to proceed without interruption. Less certainty may prompt curiosity and investigation, seeking information to restore stability to prediction.

The border between reality and prediction is monitored by consciousness, which is alert to anomalies. The unexpected event, the failure of the prediction function, sparks an inquiry. Is this something known, or is it new? If it is new, attention is focussed and the need for more information to settle the state out of incongruity to stable expectation is activated. That is curiosity. The information loop is engaged.

Prediction builds up over a lifetime. The earliest experiences of an infant of safety or neglect will colour the prediction function for the rest of their days. Intense experiences of personal threat of imminent harm or death may compromise a person's sense of safety in the world forever after. In such cases, prediction attempts to find a stable state wherein the expectation of safety, altered by a life threatening event, is balanced with constant vigilance.

Prediction works not just to build a stable model of the world around us, it builds a predictive model of everyone around us. It contains our expectations of how others will behave in a given situation. Contradictions between expected and observed behaviours may surprise us, or we may generate a narrative to explain them away or integrate them into a new understanding.

We do the same with ourselves. Our prediction function builds a model of who we believe ourselves to be. The individual memories, emotions, skills and experience stored in the unconscious all go to building a prediction of an individual persona, the entity we think of as self. It includes habits, attitudes, routines, social skills and education: everything that can be used to predict what we can expect of ourselves in most situations.

The self is an accumulation of the experiences that adds up to a description of who we are. It takes time to develop sufficient experience to form a prediction of what we, and others, might expect of ourselves. Those experiences and memories reside in an integrated form, a gestalt, in the unconscious. The predicted self is the set of guidelines and rules we believe that we live by. Like prediction for the world at large, our predicted selves constantly monitor our expected behaviour against what actually emerges in new situations. If there is a discrepancy, we may experience heightened self awareness, self consciousness or even shame.

Although in childhood the personal identity is a work in progress, as the individual grows and acquires more experience, skill and knowledge, the prediction becomes ever more detailed and compelling. The prediction can still be altered by new information. The attitudes, reactions and habitual behaviours in a predicted self can be changed with education.

The predicted self is therefore a construct of the unconscious. It is an illusion, in the way that the predicted world is a construct of the unconscious. It allows one to operate on autopilot, while dealing with the things that require scrutiny and flexibility. The concept of the self as an illusion is not new. It is a tenet of Buddhism, for example. Harris (2019) speaks eloquently to the linkage between the concepts of consciousness and the illusion of self. The loss of sense of self is an idea that arises in religion and psychiatry. The concept of a sense of self as a functioning entity is central to clinical psychology.

The predictive model is useful but we are not robots and prediction does not mean an automaton is in control. The predicted self we generate to manage routine behaviours and interactions is a very useful construct. It carries on many routine activities. This predicted self has a history, attitudes and beliefs, ways of dealing with others and the world and responding to anticipated events. It is also a cover story, some very elaborate window dressing. We may rarely see discrepancies between who we believe ourselves to be, and what our actions say about us. Then there are stories such as the one told by the neuroscientist, James Fallon in his book, *The Psychopath Inside: A Scientist's Personal Journey into the Dark Side of the Brain* (2013). He was confronted by evidence of his own psychopathic traits, which were completely discrepant with the predictive model of himself that he believed. His book is the story of how he gradually integrated the new evidence into his construct of himself.

We believe in the predicted construct of ourselves. We expect to conduct ourselves in a manner congruent with the prediction. Deviations from the prediction are explained away or dismissed. They can, but rarely, lead to major changes in the predictive model of ourselves. We live that role as though it was a full and accurate reflection of our authentic selves.

Except when it isn't, when something sufficiently unexpected perturbs us from the course and the predictive model fails. This is when we are given a glimpse into the territory behind the mirage. This is when the mask drops. The failure of prediction shows up when something unexpected occurs, but also when we explore something new. Between curiosity and random events, we are kept aware of the world around us, and ourselves. If it all gets too predictable, we go looking for something else. Curiosity may lead to new information and new information is useful to refresh the knowledge base on which prediction relies.

The predicted self may not capture real world changes accurately. If you have ever caught a glimpse of your reflection and wondered when did that change occur (greying hair, weight gain or loss, etc.) then you have experienced yourself as a prediction meeting reality. Especially as people move into middle age and beyond, they will proclaim they are "still 29 on the inside". People who suffer from eating disorders may have a very distorted image of their body shape. Have you ever heard someone insist, "I would never do such a thing" or, "I do not remember saying that, but it sounds like me". Prediction meets reality.

When prediction meets reality two things may happen: denial or attention. If there is no failure of prediction, all is as expected, then attention moves elsewhere. When reality and prediction are incongruent, attention also might be focussed on the point of discrepancy. Is there a problem that needs attention? Is there new information to be acquired?

Attention is the cognitive function of awareness, and where attention is focussed, awareness occurs. Awareness is the boundary zone between prediction and reality. Our nervous system alerts to discrepancies there, the thing that is unexpected, the thing that is new. Gut instinct, arousal of the nervous system, radar or lie detector, the names we have for these human ways all refer to the same thing: reality clashes with expectation and we are alerted. Something is – what? Different? Wrong? But it focusses our attention. We become aware.

There can be a mismatch between prediction and reality, the predicted self's behaviour, and what actually transpired. This is where you will hear the phrase, "I did not mean to do that". These behavioural discrepancies range from amusing or mildly disturbing, to deeply shocking. I have had puzzling conversations in which I point out a behaviour to someone, and the response is utter denial. If I press the point and state the evidence, the answer is sometimes a vehement, "I would never do that!". In such cases, people dismiss the behaviour and try to course correct back to the predictive model. The discrepancy needs to be reduced and the prediction and reality brought back to a stable configuration. No, I did not do that. No, that did not happen. Well, perhaps, but I did not mean for that to happen.

Awareness is the state wherein prediction and reality are held simultaneously in attention. What is experienced and what is expected are compared. The place between what should be and what is. It is the source of questions, such as, "Why did that happen?" "What is that?" "Who are you?" and "How do I make sense of this?" It also works for self awareness. "Is this who I truly am?" "That sounds like something I would do" "I would never do that" "That's not me", and "that is not something I think about". Incongruities between the two may drive the need for more information, the urge to explore, the need to investigate. Discrepancies may also drive denial. If prediction and reality are in agreement, no further action is needed. No more processing is required and no investigation or exploration is called for. The state wherein one might relax, focus on something else, rest or sleep.

Awareness is the experience of the new data in a very limited span of attention. Consciousness is a wider field in which previous learning is held in readiness, awaiting new input. It is an expectation and may take a number of forms such as an experience, a memory, a cognitive function or a motor skill. Consciousness occurs because we have accrued a fund of experience, skills and knowledge that shape a prediction of reality. Awareness occurs because we experience something new.

Self awareness is the state in which the reality of the self and the predicted self are constantly monitored. Children gradually become self aware after roughly a decade of life and this may the amount of time necessary to acquire sufficient experience to form early predictions. They are able to feel self consciousness and shame, the consequence of behaviour being incongruent with a predicted self.

In my career as a clinical neuropsychologist, I interviewed thousands of people. I tried to elicit, in one interview lasting only a few hours, a sense of their life history. What people said in that time reflected not just the problem that brought them to a neuropsychologist's office, but also what they wanted me to know about them. Like others, I came to understand that people will tell you who they are. They will also tell you who they believe they are, and the two conceptualizations can be substantially different.

There is a difference between our predicted self, the person we believe ourselves to be, and the other self that sometimes surprises us. Just like the prediction model, when that surprising discrepancy occurs, we pay attention.

When the prediction function is stable, we are able to focus on the task at hand. Perhaps we can rest. It is also when we can sleep.

There are a few things about sleep that are interesting in this context. When we want to sleep, we seek a quiet, dark place without activity. Consciousness shuts down. Things we have recently learned are strengthened and reinforced in memory during sleep. One implication is that in sleep, mental processing capacity is rerouted away from consciousness. That's a lot of processing. Perhaps the mind has to stop taking in new information so that the unconscious can properly process the day's quota of new experiences. Is this where best fit processing occurs? New paradigms built? Is this new information, given all that is already known and experienced by this individual, true or not true? Useful or not useful? Does it fit or not fit with what is already known? If all new information has to be sorted through these processes, it may look like a game of tetris going on in our heads every night.

Matthew Walker, professor of neuroscience and sleep researcher, made a similar argument in his book Why We Sleep (op cit p. 53): "When it comes to information processing, think of the wake state principally as reception (experiencing and constantly learning the world around you), NREM sleep as reflection (storing and strengthening those raw ingredients of new facts and skills), and REM sleep as integration (interconnecting these raw ingredients with each other, with all past experiences, and, in doing so, building an ever more accurate model of how the world works, including innovative insights and problem solving abilities)."

The prediction function brings a sense of certainty with it. I am quite certain the tree in front of my house is still there as I type this. I am certain that the laws of physics will continue to operate. I am certain of many things, and taken together the certainty can be characterized as a type of belief system. Some of the things that I believe to be true are idiosyncratic, particular to me and my own history. Much of the certainty is shared by others.

Belief is basically individual, a product of a single mind based on unique set of circumstances and history. Humans in groups develop a shared understanding of the world in order to act together. That shared understanding probably grows out of a number of activities, including building things together. "We tipped these big stones into holes in the ground to make them stand up. Are we all on the same page now about levers and gravity?" With group endeavours, individual belief becomes consensual reality.

A diversion now to a question about the information cycle. Most biological cycles contain forces that sustain them and keep the processes active. In the case of the information cycle, there is a constant flow of information. What drives it?

Several processes may be at work. One of those processes is asking questions. As we saw in the previous chapter, questions that are developed in the conscious mind may prompt the unconscious to a number of activities. The unconscious mind may engage functions to sort and resort information, to integrate the new information, to find an answer to the question or a better fit to the question asked. This is the situation in which the answer that comes to mind is not new information, but information already known presented in a new configuration. The unconscious does not tell you anything new, it tells you what you already know in a different pattern.

Curiosity is another process that prompts investigation and exploration. Investigating the unknown can turn up the unexpected, and the unexpected represents a failure of prediction. A failure of prediction brings attention and awareness, and the need to reconcile what should be with what is. A failure of prediction seeks not just additional information but also an effort to bring the awareness / prediction boundary back to a stable state. This might require an adjustment to the prediction.

Once something such as a procedure or skill is acquired and routinized, it fades from awareness. That leaves awareness with nothing upon which to focus. We ask ourselves, what's next? Humans are hard wired to respond to novelty. Anything new will kickstart the cycle.

Another process is uncertainty. Information in the unconscious is sorted and stacked into the most stable configurations, the ones that have the greatest probability of accurately prediction the real world. This is the basis of prediction, and it carries with it into awareness a sense of certainty. The predicted world is the real world. Other configurations are less certain and carry with them an air of possibility rather than certainty, and these we think of as ideas. Some ideas have much less certainty and bring with them a sense of doubt. The latter two cases spur action to resolve uncertainty and bring the reality prediction into greater stability. The action might be investigation or dismissal. "I wonder if that will work" compared to "That will never work".

Another process might occur in the social interactions wherein information is shared, skills are taught and learned, ideas are discussed and stories told. Before we have our individual prediction machinery built up, we rely on the older and more experienced members of our social group to teach us how the world works. The process of sharing what we know amongst ourselves continues through the lifetime.

What does it look like when the information cycle slows or falters? It may look like the cognitive changes in Alzheimer's disease and depression. One sees a dulling in the facial expression, declining memory function, slowed movements and apathy. A lack of curiosity is also seen when thinking has become closed or rigid. If one is certain about everything all of the time there is little room for new learning. Finally, insufficient environmental stimulation can cause much harm to a developing minds and adults alike. Neglect, imprisonment and isolation are toxic environments.

There is a constant dynamic in the ongoing comparison between expected and experience. This is where under stimulation, insufficient change or novelty, results in boredom, tedium and restlessness. The cognitive juncture between expectation and reality is set for optimal levels of stimulus. Too much or too little is uncomfortable and unproductive. At optimum levels, this is the experience of being alive. It is the place of being fully conscious, alert and aware.

When I first started on this book I thought of the unconscious as a mystery. Just one big, strange, black hole. What I failed to understand is that, although the conscious mind does not have direct, intentional access to the contents of the unconscious, there is another way to think of it. We can not directly access the unconscious mind, but we can be receptive when it shows itself. We can learn to pay attention.

Unconscious information shows up constantly in the conscious mind in the form of expectation, ideas, memories, inspiration, guesses, artistic and creative work. The conscious mind, in its stream of consciousness way, has its own form of internal chatter. In my head the chatter is in words, storylines and dialogue. I carry on unspoken conversations, watch scenarios unfold and predict who will say and do what. It is all narrative. I have a friend who paints and has superb colour sense. I imagine much of her internal dialogue is shape and colour, placement and arrangement. I asked a former teaching assistant who was doing her master's degree in English literature what was the point of literature. I was younger and thinking of career options in science at the time and so perhaps the silliness of the question could be overlooked. As though explaining the use of alphabets, she said, "Because that is how one organizes the world". This internal conversation is spoken by the conscious mind and fueled by the unconscious. The interchange of organizing concepts, information, thoughts and ideas is constant. The unconscious is always with our conscious minds.

It is rather like saying that I can not pinpoint where the breeze is coming from, but I can feel it on my face.

*****

In the end, consciousness is still an endlessly interesting problem. As I heard speakers at MAIN2021 (2021), a neurosciences and consciousness forum, recently confess, much data on brain activity is collected but it is not clear what it means. We are still trying to build useful models of consciousness. This book takes the approach of asking how consciousness might function as part of an information processing cycle.

The book proposes that the human mind operates a dedicated information processing system. It operates in two phases, conscious and unconscious. Consciousness is one phase in an information processing cycle, and the goal of that system is learning. For our human minds, information is just raw sensory data that can be processed into its various spatial, linguistic, sensory and motor components. That information is placed into a personal context where it becomes meaningful, where it makes sense in light of other information. At that point information becomes knowledge. It is a remarkably effective system for gathering and organizing information. For a creature with no armour or poisonous sting, that is relatively puny and weak in the overall scheme of things, the human capacity to acquire information, transform and use it, is adaptive. Knowledge is power.

Chapter 11: Summary

Consciousness is not a thing, it is one phase in a cognitive cycle that processes information. The unconscious is not a mysterious dark cave, it is another phase of the cycle. The conscious phase of this cycle is familiar territory. In neuropsychology, it is the part of the process we investigate. The different functions that are active in this phase, attention, sensation, motor, visuospatial, language, memory, executive, all go into the work of sensing raw environmental data and processing it.

The unconscious phase is less easily understood. It is not available to the conscious processes of investigation and analysis, and this reflects the fundamental nature of the cycle of information processing. Each phase has dedicated tasks and tools in the information processing cycle and a wide band of awareness is not one of them in the conscious phase. The conscious mind can not peer directly into the unconscious phase. The unconscious phase can not speak directly to the conscious mind in the language the conscious mind uses. Of course we would like to know more, but those avenues are indirect. Each phase is structured for other activities.

The conscious mind has the curious capacity to compare real world data to the predictions fed forward by the unconscious phase. Holding prediction and reality simultaneously in the function of attention sets up a condition wherein several forms of the same thing exist together, and these create a specialized state of awareness. It is not unlike when separate beams of light integrate into a three dimensional hologram.

The mind already has mechanisms in place that compare two sets of similar, but not identical data and generate a third condition. When both eyes compare sensory data of the same object, an algorithm integrates the subtle differences and creates the experience of three dimensional vision. A comparison of the sensory data of sound heard in two ears permits accurate determination of the source of the sound. A third quality is generated from two similar but not identical inputs. It is a mechanism that suggests itself to the question of awareness.

The nature and contents of the unconscious store of information is a tantalizing problem. The task of the conscious mind is to acquire information. The unconscious is a potential store of inaccessible information. The curious and exploring conscious phase is not going to leave that problem alone.

The work of Owen (2017) and Gazzaniga (1988) indicates that seemingly non conscious or nonverbal aspects of mind are aware of the real world, and understand the language, such as English, that the conscious mind uses. This unconscious phase of mind does not speak directly to the conscious phase in, for convenience let us say, English, but information is nonetheless transmitted from one phase to the next.

So, how does this information transfer occur? What language does the unconscious speak?

Different fields have developed tools that can be used to glean information. Psychoanalysis will consider the symbolic meaning of dreams. Clinical psychology considers the implications of hidden motivators on behaviour. Neuropsychology considers the change in information that may arise after consolidation in long term memory.

There are also the spontaneous communications that emerge in the conscious mind in the form of predicted reality, ideas, inspirations, solutions to problems and the coming together of disparate pieces into a whole, a gestalt.

This leads to another interesting question. One task of the unconscious mind is to provide a running prediction of what we can expect when we consciously interact with the world. The unconscious mind provides a working version of reality for the conscious phase. It tells us what is real. The spontaneous emergence in consciousness of something else in addition to prediction opens up another question. What is it that the unconscious phase communicates to the conscious mind? What does it wants you to know?

Commonly, awareness in the conscious phase is an alert to incongruities, the situation in which prediction and real world data do not match up. When the conscious mind can respond, it does. If the conscious mind can not, for any reason, respond by becoming aware of the incongruity, the unconscious nonetheless communicates with a signal of nonverbal sensation. This is the 'best guess' of blindsight patients, pointing to a dot of light they do not know they see. This is the sense of unease or fear of which DeBecker (1993) speaks.

This is also the territory of curiosity, when the conscious mind is made aware of missing information. The unconscious signals that the sorting and integrating process is stymied by lack of information to achieve a best fit solution.

The unconscious phase will also communicate insight, that point when pieces of information have been tightly sorted and achieve a 'best fit' status. This is the experience of understanding. It is the "I get it now" or "it all makes sense" moment.

The unconscious phase not only understands language, it seeks to answer questions posed in the language of the conscious mind. This may be the disconnected right hemisphere pointing to pictures it has seen (Gazzaniga, 1988). It may also be the visualization of walking or hitting a tennis ball described by Owen (2017). It is the sudden awareness of an answer to a problem described by Sacks (2017). This may be why we say problems can be solved by asking the right question.

This opens up another interesting question. Is it possible for the conscious mind to communicate more efficiently with the unconscious phase? Can we 'learn the language' of the unconscious? If the unconscious phase is processing information, thereby carrying out cognitive processes, there might be avenues that neuropsychology and cognitive psychology can explore.

The first steps in any field study, like field walking in archaeology, are to gather observations and consider models.

The unconscious phase is constantly communicating with the conscious phase, predominantly in the form of prediction. The unconscious phase not only understands language, it reads the environment constantly. We thinks of this in terms of incidental learning, and we used to speak of subliminal perception. The unconscious is working on all of the information it can obtain, through direct awareness, incidental observation and all of the experiences and skills acquired in its lifetime. It will, when needed, offer up the next steps in a motor sequence or the next logical step in a rational process such as chess or development of a scientific hypothesis. It may ask for more information or more analysis by sparking the sense of curiosity.

When the unconscious is communicating, it does so in a manner that reveals its methods of communicating, its language if you will. Whereas the conscious mind analyzes and breaks down information into categories by cognitive domain plus motor function plus sensation plus emotion, the unconscious processes, sorts and integrates information from all these sources. What comes back to our conscious mind is literally transformed and not easily experienced as language. It is an amalgam bound together with meaning, and that can be read as emotion, or a meaningful, logical cognitive assembly such as physics, or perhaps as shapes, colours and location in space when you see it in your mind's eye. When information circulates from the unconscious phase into the conscious phase, it is in the form of a meaningful assembly. The unconscious works to build a stable, reliable gestalt.

The attribute of meaning added in this part of the cycle also reflects the priorities of the unconscious phase. Rote learning is not a priority and is easily lost. Information that holds little or no meaning, such as what you ate for dinner last Tuesday, may be easily lost. The expression on your partner's face at your wedding may never be lost. Memory of any kind, spontaneous or effortful, accurate or erroneous, factual or emotional, reflects the priorities of the information processing cycle at work. Some information is lost and this is a reflection of the unconscious making a determination of value. Motor skills, responses to threatening situations, speaking and locating, are higher priority activities and they are less likely to degrade in the normal course of events than, for example, the location of one's car keys.

The unconscious does not communicate in a language such as English because its' main function is to take information and organize it as tightly and coherently as it can, in order to provide best quality reality predictions to the conscious mind. Its' communication mode, if there is one, is a complex set of information connected in a composite of images, sensations, emotions, motor functions and words. It understands the cognitive modalities fed to it by the conscious mind, but it does not preferentially use them to communicate with the conscious mind because that is not its job. Integrated sets of data, of mixed forms, is what it builds and what it has to offer.

The conscious mind seeks experiences, information and skills. The unconscious mind binds those elements into a meaningful whole in order to create the most reliable and accurate prediction possible. The cycle operates in phases of light and shadow, conscious and unconscious. The cycle processes information, and the goal is learning.

REFERENCES

Ajina, S., & Bridge, H. (2017) Blindsight and unconscious vision: What they teach us about the human visual system. *The Neuroscientist*, 23(5), pp. 529–541.

Baars, B. J. (2005) Global workspace theory of consciousness: Toward a cognitive neuroscience of human experience, in Laurey, S. (ed.) *Progress in Brain Research*, 150, pp. 45–53. Elsevier.

Baars, B. J. (2017). The Global Workspace Theory of Consciousness: Predictions and Results. In S. Schneider & M. Velmans (Eds.), *The Blackwell Companion to Consciousness* (pp. 227–242). John Wiley & Sons, Ltd. https://doi.org/10.1002/9781119132363.ch16

Bargh, J. A. (2017) Before you know it: The unconscious reasons we do what we do. *New York, Touchstone.*

Bargh, J. A., & Morsella, E. (2008) The unconscious mind. *Perspectives on Psychological Science*, 3(1), pp. 73–79.

Barrett, L. F. (2020). *Seven and a half lessons about the brain*. Boston, Houghton Mifflin Harcourt.

Berry, W. (1981). Solving for Pattern. Chapter 9 in *The gift of good land: Further essays, cultural and agricultural*. North Point Press.

Chabris, C. & Simons D. (2010) The invisible gorilla: How our intuitions deceive us. Crown Publishing, Penguin Random House.

De Becker, Gavin (1997) The gift of fear: Survival signals that protect us from violence. Dell Publishing, New York, New York.

Diener, E. & Biswas-Diener, R. (2021). The replication crisis in psychology. In R. Biswas-Diener & E. Diener (Eds), Noba textbook series: Psychology. Champaign, IL: DEF publishers. Retrieved from http://noba.to/q4cvydeh

Fallon, J. H. (2013). *The psychopath inside: A neuroscientist's personal journey into the dark side of the brain*. The Penguin Group, USA.

Gazzaniga, M. S. (1988). *Mind matters: How mind and brain interact to create our conscious lives*. Boston, Houghton Mifflin ; Published in association with the MIT Press.

Goodglass, H., Klein, B., Carey, P., & Jones, K. (1966). Specific Semantic Word Categories in Aphasia. *Cortex*, 2(1), 74–89.

Gopnik, A., O'Grady, S., Lucas, C.G., Griffiths, T.L., Wente, A., Bridgers, S., Aboody, R., Fung, H. and Dahl, R.E. "Changes in Cognitive Flexibility and Hypothesis Search across Human Life History from Childhood to Adolescence to Adulthood." *Proceedings of the National Academy of Sciences* 114, no. 30 (July 25, 2017): 7892–99. https://doi.org/10.1073/pnas.1700811114.

Gopnik, A. "Childhood as a Solution to Explore–Exploit Tensions." *Philosophical Transactions of the Royal Society B: Biological Sciences* 375, no. 1803 (July 20, 2020): 20190502. https://doi.org/10.1098/rstb.2019.0502.

Harris, A. (2019). *Conscious: A brief guide to the fundamental mystery of the mind* (First edition). New York, Harper, an imprint of HarperCollinsPublishers.

Holmes, G. (1918) Disturbances of vision by cerebral lesions. *The British Journal of Ophthalmology*, 2, pp. 353–384.

Kahneman, D. (2011). *Thinking, fast and slow* (1st ed). Doubleday Canada.

Kihlstrom, J. F. (1987). The cognitive unconscious. *Science*, 237 (18 September 1987), pp. 1445–1452.

Koriat, A. (2000). The feeling of knowing: Some metatheoretical implications for consciousness and control. *Consciousness and Cognition*, 9(2), 149–171. https://doi.org/10.1006/ccog.2000.0433

Loftus, E. F., & Pickrell, J. E. (1995). The formation of false femories. *Psychiatric Annals*, *25*(12), 720–725. https://doi.org/10.3928/0048-5713-19951201-07

MAIN 2021 (2021) Montreal AI & Neuroscience. https://www.main2021.org/home

Karim Jerbi. (2021, November 29). *Opening remarks MAIN 2021*. MAIN 2021, Montreal.

McCartney, Paul (author) and Muldoon, Paul (editor) (2021) The Lyrics. Liveright, W.W. Norton Books, New York, New York.

McGilchrist, I. (2019). The master and his emissary: The divided brain and the making of the western world *(New expanded edition). Yale University Press.*

Miller, G. A. (1956). The magical number seven, plus or minus two: Some limits on our capacity for processing information. *Psychological Review*, *63*(2), 81–97.

Nisbett, R. E., & Wilson, T. D. (1977) Telling more than we can know: Verbal reports on mental processes. Psychological Review, 84(3), pp. 231–259.

Owen, A. M. (2017). Into the gray zone: A neuroscientist explores the border between life and death (First Scribner hardcover edition). New York, Scribner.

Pally, R. (2005) Non-conscious prediction and a role for consciousness in correcting prediction errors. *Cortex*, 41(5), pp. 643–662.

Pearson, P. (2014). Opening heaven's door: Investigating stories of life, death, and what comes after. *Random House, Toronto, Canada.*

Ramachandran, V. S., & Blakeslee, S. (1998) Phantoms in the brain: Probing the mysteries of the human mind. New York, William Morrow.

Sacks, Oliver (2017) The river of consciousness. New York, *Alfred A. Knopf.*

Schacter, D. L. (1983). Feeling of knowing in episodic memory. Journal of Experimental Psychology: Learning, Memory, and Cognition, 9(1), 39–54. https://doi.org/10.1037/0278-7393.9.1.39

Schacter DL. "The Seven Sins of Memory." *American Psychologist* 54, no. 3 (March 1999): 182–203.

Schacter, D., McAndrews, M.P. And Moscovitch, M. (1988) Access to consciousness: Dissociations between implicit and explicit knowledge in neuropsychological syndromes. In Weiskrantz, L. (ed.) *Thought Without Language*, New York: Oxford University Press.

Sperry, R. (1977). *Consciousness, personal identity, and the divided brain.* Frank Nelson Doubleday Lecture Series, Smithsonian Institution.

Steeves, P. F. C. (2021). *The indigenous paleolithic of the western hemisphere.* Lincoln, University of Nebraska Press.

Walker, M. P. (2017). *Why we sleep: Unlocking the power of sleep and dreams.* (First Scribner hardcover edition). Scribner, an imprint of Simon & Schuster, Inc.

Weiskrantz, L. (2004) Roots of blindsight. *Progress in Brain Research*, 144, pp. 229–241.

Wilson, T. D. (2002) Strangers to ourselves: Discovering the adaptive unconscious. *Belknap Press of Harvard University Press.*